Letters to my *Daughter*

Copyright © Laura Elizabeth
First published in Australia in 2022
by Maven Press
Roleystone WA 6111

Cover Design by Kristy Jamieson

Edited by Jade Bell

All rights reserved. No part of this book may be used or reproduced by any means, graphic, electronic, or mechanical, including photocopying, recording, taping or by any information storage retrieval system without the written permission of the copy¬right owner except in the case of brief quotations embodied
in critical articles and reviews.

Because of the dynamic nature of the Internet, any web addresses or links contained in this book may have changed since publication and may no longer be vaild. The views expressed in this work are solely those of the author and do not necessarily reflect the views of the publisher and the publisher hereby disclaims
any responsibility for them.

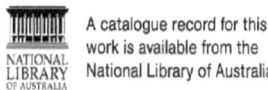

National Library of Australia Catalogue-in-Publication data:

Letters to my Daughter/Laura Elizabeth

ISBN: 978-0-6453230-6-1

(Paperback)

ISBN: 978-0-6453230-7-8

(Ebook)

Acknowledgements

In unity, we honour and pay our respects to the custodians of Whadjuk Noongar Boodjar country, the lands on which this book was first seeded.

We pay our respects to the Elders both past and present
and to those emerging.
The stories within these pages may contain sensitive content and/or
memories of loved ones who have passed on,
which may activate a response within you.

Please read with awareness and care.

Letters to my Daughter

Lisa Bito	7
Freyja Stone	10
Heidi Mippy	12
Lisa Bito	15
Karen McDermott	18
Rebecca Lee	20
Haylee Guiver	24
Rachel Carmichael	26
Sarah Montgomery	28
Hayley French	32
Laura Elizabeth	34
Janice Cooper	36
Nellie Barnett	39
Briony J	42
Alysha Christensen	45
Nicole Aly	48
Trish Bond	51
Chantelle Dawn Skye	54
Dawn Mills	57

Ashlea Carpenter	59
Fiona Dyer	62
Lauren Maslin	64
Fiona Cartledge	66
Tanya Morriss	69
Ashleigh Moreland	71
Jessica Russell	74
Rebekah Rose	77
Melissa Lainer	79
Cymon Cox	81
Kate Billen	83
Cassey Crook	85
Rachael Bryden	88
Shelley Brown	90
Gezzell Sabina	92
Belle Verdiglione	94
Raylene Joiner	96
Jenny Arnold	98
Conny Wladkowski	101
Tracey Wilson	103
Aimee Mitchell	106
Emma Fedigan	109
Amanda Scott	112
Jenny Stanley-Matthews	113
Kristie Inker	116
Marie Czatyrko	118
A Letter to your Daughter	121

Letters to my Daughter

Lisa Bito

I Want You to Know

Lisa Bito

You are loved. Deeply loved and deeply held by all those around you—me, your dad, your siblings, grandparents, ancestors, friends, everyone.

The light will always find you, even on the darkest days. It may be the smallest sliver, but if you look, it's there. So don't ever stop believing there is light, even at the end of the darkest tunnel.

Do you—each and every moment of every day. Even if it means you don't conform, even if it means you challenge me or others, or even if it means you disappoint. Stand in your truth and in your power. Find these things and stay in them always. The journey to your truth and power may be long but keep searching no matter what.

You will love, you will lose, you will hurt others, you will be hurt, and you will be full of the extremes of happiness and sadness. Each emotion, experience and feeling is valid and deserves its voice. Feel them all and let them work their way through you. Hold on to the ones you need and let the others go. They will ebb and flow like water, like Mother Nature and her seasons. Let them.

Live a life of passion and purpose. Find those two things in your soul and make them your life's journey.

Find the things, people, places and experiences that light up your soul and hold them close. Cherish them. Rejoice in them. Spend your entire life finding the moments where your soul is lit up by fireworks.

Letters to my Daughter

Revel in each and every experience. Some will bring joy, some will bring tears, but every single one is worth experiencing.

Don't wait to be saved by the prince in the fairy tale. That's all it is—a fairy tale that bears no resemblance to real life. Life is not like a Disney movie. Instead, teach yourself the skills you need. You don't need to be saved by anyone. You can save yourself.

Love yourself and love your body. Your body is a temple. Learn to worship it with a deeply held reverence for all it does for you and how it carries you through life. Love sits at the centre of the universe. It's why we exist. And you can't love someone fully until you love and accept yourself. That includes your body. It's designed for so many powerful things. It's a receptacle for pleasure. Don't spend your time and energy starving it, abusing it and mistreating it. When you abuse your body, you abuse yourself. And you need to love yourself. No one can love you the way you can, and you deserve to love yourself.

Be a woman of strength—physical, mental, emotional and spiritual. Be a warrior, slay those dragons and stand in your full power. But keep your soft edges. They soften the power with love.

Find your pack. Make sure every person in your life is on your side. If they're not, be strong enough to say goodbye. You deserve a support crew who loves and respects you and has your back every time. Listen to their counsel with wise, discerning ears, even if it makes you uncomfortable and shows your shadow. They speak with love. Don't undersell yourself to anyone. If they don't treat you right, have the strength to walk out the door.

Do the things that scare the shit out of you. Step outside your fear and comfort zone. You don't grow if you never blur the lines. Live your life outside your comfort zone, stretching yourself. Believe in yourself and what you can do. You can achieve anything you set your mind to.

Believe in magic. It surrounds you. See the magic and wonder everywhere and sprinkle a bit wherever you go.

Be compassionate and kind, always. Try and hold compassion and love for those that hurt you. The pain they inflict says more about them than you. Try and remember this even when it's hard.

Forgive.

Forgiveness is a skill that's fucking hard to learn but try. I'm not asking you to forget, but learn to forgive. It goes hand in hand with love and compassion and will leave you with a full heart.

Be financially independent. Enough said!

Set boundaries. Work out the things that matter to you and the limits you will accept. Set boundaries around those and don't waver from them.

Use your fucking voice!

Find your voice and use it. Don't waste fifty years of your life watering yourself down to please others. Don't keep quiet about the things that matter to you. Find that voice inside you, shout it out loud and stand proud. Be the person I was too scared to be. Don't live your life bound by fear.

Letters to my Daughter

Sacred Flow

Freyja Stone

I dreamt of you long before we met. Thank you for choosing me. I feel so blessed to be your Mumma. Nothing in this life is permanent except my love for you.

Life is a crazy ride. Shit is going to happen. You will make mistakes. You will fall, and you will rise. Some people will love you, and some will inevitably hurt you. What's important is the alchemy. It's what you do with it all that matters. The power lies in the ability to see the lesson in each situation, especially those that hurt.

May you have the gift to allow the flow, to allow yourself to feel and release with ease and move on with only love in your heart.

Everyone is a teacher, and you are my greatest teacher yet.

Always stay true to yourself. Some will try and tell you how to live and tell you who you are. Your life is your story and yours alone, and you are the only one that can make you happy. Happiness is an inside job. You are and always will be the most important person in your life.

BE MORE SELFISH!

You can be kind and loving and still have solid boundaries—practice self-love. Keep your dreams to yourself, don't allow others to burden you with their doubts and limitations.

The only opinion that matters is yours. It's not your business what others think, nor does it matter.

Always choose you. The most valuable thing you can do is understand yourself and your needs and wants.

Find the things that make you happy.

Freyja Stone

Live with intention and integrity, set boundaries, and get comfortable saying no. Stand in your truth, read, create, travel, reflect, explore and grow.

Practice acceptance and living without attachment. Learn when it's time to let go, forgive and flow.

There is an ocean of endless possibilities awaiting you. EVERYTHING is possible.

There will be times when you will feel lost, but in our darkest moments, we often find our truth. In this time, you can come back to your heart space, set sacred space, and sit with whatever it is. Honour your sacredness. You are exactly enough, and you are worthy, so worthy. Remind yourself that everything will work out for your highest good.

To gain clarity, we must open ourselves to the possibility of change, get uncomfortable, explore our shadows, take a risk, be vulnerable, and permit ourselves to sit in this space. It creates space where the magic happens. We ask questions, and the universe answers with new possibilities, unexpected opportunities, inspiration and direction. We flow.

Even in the darkest of times, she kept reaching for the light
Holding the secrets of the universe within her hear
Walking into the unknown with faith shown on the way
Never steering off her path because guidance was never far away
The wind whooshing around her, the water showing her how to flow, the fire igniting her inner warrior and the earth bringing her home
For she would keep searching and exploring
Turning her stories into gifts for those she connects with on the way
Gifts of creation, freedom and hope
Continuously she rewrites her story to align with her truth. She transformed her pain into art and let go of anything that didn't belong to her
Enjoying the mystery & the unfolding while anticipating what was to come next.

Letters to my Daughter

My Daughters I love You

Heidi Mippy

To My Daughters,
   Each of you is a unique, beautiful, and amazing being with individual personalities and traits that make you who you are.
   I love each of you equally and deeper than the ocean.
   As you read this letter, I want you to embrace what I have written. I hope these words touch your hearts and reach the places needed.
   I hope you can hear my voice and feel my love every time you read these words knowing that I am right here by your side and always will be.

I love you

   I want to tell you, my daughters, that even though we have lived alone most of our lives, you need to know that your father loves you as deeply as I do. I know this because I have felt the love from your father and know how good his heart is. I know this because you were each made from the unity of love. The love between your father and me was real, but as you will learn over time, love doesn't last forever, and it changes as people change.
   My relationship with your father and his relationship with me does not reflect our love for you. We will always love you, and you will always be our babies, and from that, you should draw strength, pride, and love for who you are. Never doubt our love for you or the love I have for you. You stand

on the shoulders of giants. Always be proud of who you are, knowing the strength of our bloodlines run through you.

Live and learn

I have raised you to be strong. I have done this because I know how cruel the world can be. I taught you strength so you could withstand the harshest of life's lessons, the people you will cross with an ugly heart, and unfair moments you will struggle to understand. I raised you strong because although we belong to the world's longest surviving culture and stand proud and tall in who we are, we are often misunderstood and manipulated. You will be racially profiled every day, facing systemic oppression and racism, and it will hurt. It will cut deep.

A mother feels her child's pain, and I have felt the pain I know you will face. So I have raised you strong. You will be a survivor, a warrior, and in time a great matriarch for our family, like the giants of the shoulders you stand on. I have armed you with knowledge that will help you understand who you are and why the world is as it is. I have armed you with the strength to stand in your power, to be proud.

But this, my daughters, doesn't mean you cannot show weakness. The fact is, my girls, you don't get the light without the dark! Don't ever be afraid of the dark, for you have the strength to find your way back to the light. You have the spirits of your old people always by your side, and in the moments when you think you are ready to go deeper into the dark, they will pull you out. We will pull you out, and your heart will feel whole again.

I am proud of you

There are people in life who will do everything they can to write your story for you. They will tell you who they think you are and who you should be. They will ask you to fol, and they will ask you to lead. They will set expectations for you, but you know your limits, and it is up to you to strive beyond them.

Be brave, my daughters, and never be afraid to shine your light and guide your path. You know who you are. You are guided by some of the

Letters to my Daughter

most powerful and wisest matriarchs that ever walked this earth. You will always receive a sign to remind you of their presence. They will give you a push forward or slap you in the face and make you stop. But at the end of the day, it is you who will make the choices, and I will always be proud of you. Some of your choices won't be the best, but they are still important. They each bring learning and experience and are but a chapter of your story.

Keep writing.
Choose your own adventure.
Be you.

Love and Laugh

Life is too short isn't a saying to encourage you to race to some imaginary finish line or reach a destination. It's a reminder to live in the moment. Enjoy every day. Be awake on your journey. Love deeply and unconditionally.

Do not fear love. You will have your heart broken many times, but when your heart sings, it will sing so loud, and you will dance like nobody is watching. You will begin to see who fills your cup and who empties it. Be grateful for all the good things in life, and don't take anything for granted.

Laugh at yourself and laugh with others. Don't underestimate the power of laughter, and remember those moments when you felt embraced by a warm hug and a loving smile. Remember the love and laughter that you girls have shared and how strong the bond of sisterhood is. When I think of this, I will forever have the image of you three girls, each with a pair of undies on your head laughing uncontrollably. That, my girls, is love.

I will always love you.

Lisa Bito

A Letter to Struggle

Lisa Bito

I see you in your struggle. I see you in your doubts. I see the abuse you land on your body unwittingly. Each time you look in the mirror, I see the lack of depth in your own self-worth. The false images constantly flashing before your eyes on social media and television, the pressure from society to look and act a certain way. The unrealistic comparison to people who also have their own demons, issues, and lack of self-worth but are putting on a front, a mask to the world to hide their own insecurities. Dumping their insecurities on a whole generation of impressionable teenagers who are struggling to find their voice and worth. Perpetuating a cycle that has gone on for women through the ages.

I see the pain you struggle with and the constant battle in your mind as the voices of the demons who deny you to eat win. Your heart knows what it needs to do, but the voices are strong, so strong they drown out the voices from your heart and the voices of the people who care about you. I know you hear my words and the words of the people trying to help you, but those voices inside your head are incessant. Persistent and unrelenting, and so far winning the battle for your attention, although I feel the sheer strength of you is turning the tide.

But I also see the depths of your character, the deep well of your absolute beauty. Not skin-deep beauty, but the beauty that shines through you, your essence. A gorgeous soul full of love, compassion and empathy. The inner strength of your being, the potential that will envelop the world in a glow of white light radiating from your soul. You have little knowledge of that person yet, but they will reveal themselves to you like jewels, treasures to

Letters to my Daughter

be unearthed. So brilliantly sparkling, each facet uncovered as your belief in yourself and your depth builds.

I wish you could see through my eyes the magnificent, powerful woman I see when I look at you. You are gorgeous on the outside, but more importantly, you are gorgeous on the inside. And that's the person I don't want you to forget is at your core as we travel this road together, however long this particular journey lasts.

Your strength of character is not a mystery to me, but I know at the moment it's buried beneath layers of earth waiting to be excavated. I hope you see the value in digging through these layers and finding your inner gold. I will hold your hand as each nugget comes to the surface, each one revealed if you are willing and ready to sit in one of the hardest things you will do. Sit in your sadness, sit in the depths of your dislike and unworthiness.

All you need to remember is the *'you'* the people who love you see, and that your pack will be alongside you every step of the way. We will chant on the sidelines, bolstering you when you need it and sitting with you on the darkest days, just holding space and shining love back into you.

The pain that has lodged in your heart does not have to stay. The tangled cobwebs that enmesh you do not need to keep you stuck forever. The procession of unworthy thoughts do not have to stay lodged in your brain. Let your pack and I help you with the things holding you back.

My wish for you on this journey is that you are brave enough to be strong, be independent, be powerful, be gentle, be kind, be compassionate, be fierce, be full of love and be willing to give and receive. Be whoever you want to be but just be you.

Do you each and every day of your life. Find you deep within and do you. Be the true authentic you. I know this is the biggest struggle for you at the moment but believe that we around you see those qualities inside you. Be brave enough to bring these to the surface. Don't let where you're currently sitting define you for the rest of your life.

There is a spark. A spark buried inside you. Let it ignite and burn bright. Let it burn fiercely, so fiercely that it dims all the outside noise. Keep that fire lit, keep that fire bright. That spark in your heart is you, your essence, your guiding light. That's what keeps you alive, keeps you magic, keeps you burning bright, so make sure you keep it alight. Fight

Lisa Bito

to keep it alive. Don't let those voices screaming in your head douse that spark. You can't see it at the moment but the light is there. Never doubt its existence.

Reach out to us, reach out to me and we will help you find it.

I see the current pain but I also see the beauty and the treasure.

We will make sure they win out.

Letters to my Daughter

For My Girls

Karen McDermott

To my four girls,

Being your mum is the biggest joy of my life. Yes, we have tough days, and Mary, goodness you are a tornado, but I learn something new about myself every day from each of you and feel blessed that you chose me to be your mum.

I would love to share with you some of the essence of my connection with my mum so that you can have a deeper understanding of life and its potential.

I am the eldest in my family. I came after my parents lost a child. As you know, you all came after I lost twins. I never knew my heart could hold so much love until you were all born, and I thank you for helping me fill the void that loss brings.

I was gifted unconditional love from my parents, I had the freedom to explore life and make mistakes, and when I tripped or fell over, I had a safe haven to retreat to and a non-judgemental embrace there. Because I was able to be curious, I had a deeper connection to myself and never felt that I was missing out on life. We were not the wealthiest family, and as I was the first of six children, I watched the dynamics of our family change as each child was born, but the one thing that did not change was the unconditional love.

As I grew older, I became aware that not everyone grew up with love as a foundation to life, and through love, children flourish. It is my hope that you come to appreciate and feel that you have been loved from the moment you were conceived.

Karen McDermott

When I would have a problem and would go to my mum for advice, her answer would always be the same 'Karen, do whatever it is that makes you happy'.

Yes, it is as simple as that in my mother's eyes, and as I grow older, I realise that it is as simple as that! We need to prioritise joy in our lives because when we do, we beam a ray of light.

Know that having material things is lovely and helps you create opulent energy, but true happiness comes from within. The feeling you feel when you know that you are exactly in the right place for your right now, and that you can tap into the unlimited well of the loving energy source you have inside. That is where true wealth resides.

I have many takeaways from life and how I choose to live it. I know that life is so much more than what is right in front of you. Choose to understand the Universal laws and work with them, and you will experience flow.

Understand that you will feel out of your comfort zone when you are pursuing something bigger than yourself. But take a moment to embrace that a lot of life's magic happens outside of your comfort zone. If you channel all decisions through your natural-born ability to *Know* then you will never fail. When you learn how to *Know*, you will be able to make decisions with unwavering faith that you are moving towards your highest potential.

I hope that you have the opportunity in your life to feel the divine feeling that is being aligned with your highest potential and love your life, just the way it is. I often walk out onto our patio and feel true love-fuelled gratitude for the love I feel in my heart for my life.

Not many people get to experience this in their lifetime. The key is to prioritise Love and Joy in your life.

Love life, and it will love you back.

Love always, Mum xxx.

Letters to my Daughter

Poems for my Daughter
Rebecca Lee

Womb Space

Linings and layers. Intrinsically tied.
My Womb Space bears the scars I hide.

Beneath skin surface, expose! Be Warned!
A plethora of fissures, fragmented, malformed.

Sustenance of lineage brings great demise.
Not undulation, but typhoon tides.

Bucketed shelter, a dark moon falls.
My daughter carries forward to be forewarned.

Resting place of my lover's seed.
Return the spark of life to me.

Rebecca Lee

As Long As Love Is Creeping In

I lay in quiet tones
with the gentle strumming of her breath
slumber in breaking the darkness
under woollen threads.

A snuggle on a shared pillow
tucked in space and time
cuddles with my daughter
makes this mother's heart shine.

Wrapped around my neck
is the youngest cubs paw
cocooned in a dreamlike state
growing his lion's roar.

Sun is breaking through
the rusted window framed
rain patters lightly
roofed upon my frail tin.

I care not of the walls around us
as long as love is creeping in.

Letters to my Daughter

Rabbit Hole

My daughter isn't she just the sweetest. Please and thank you always. Pardon and excuse. Manners are impeccable.

She knows her place in the world because I always remind her.
'DO NOT raise your voice to me. You may give rise to revolution.'
'DO NOT dare to dream. The glass ceiling is far too fragile.'

No!

Burrow yourself a rabbit hole deep into the earth. You're far too cute to be displaying rage up here. Leave all that big thinking down there. You don't want to waste it on deaf ears. You don't want to waste time to aspire.

When you emerge, make sure you wash off that dirt. You should smell like a flower. Pretty as a button with a pink bow in your hair. You are just the most perfect, sweetest LITTLE thing.

Rebecca Lee

Fires of Transformation

I have resolved to model for my daughter how to walk
gracefully through fires of transformation.

It is not only for her. It is a declaration to all
lineage her womb space bares.

My job is not to save her from the blaze. Although,
that was my belief in the beginning.
I was ashamed that I did not carry the light while I
carried her. The reprieve is that it's never too late.

Ashes to ashes, or so they say. So what difference is to be made?

The answer, my friend, is indifference. A lack of intent!

Should we start the spark and walk away? Or tend to kindle the flame?

We should not stand idle in the dark! The warm
glow should penetrate our bones.

We should be dancing. Barefoot. Naked. We are surrounded by
the souls we have a healthy binding to—those past and present.

Play with the fire, my little gypsy one.
I will teach you how to protect your skin.

Letters to my Daughter

My Beautiful Daughter

Haylee Quiver

To my daughter,

    I discovered your presence deep within my womb space. You were barely a speck, but I saw you. I saw my belly growing, creating a warm-safe home for you to morph, stretch and kick.

    I imagine you are born with soft, delicate skin, unblemished and unscarred.

    I will trace my fingertips along your skin as you sleep, leaving invisible lines of adoration, my pride in creating something so beautiful melts through my touch.

    I place my hand lightly over your chest, feeling the rise and fall of your breath.

    Toddlerhood will bring beautiful rolls along your arms and legs We will blow raspberries on your skin to hear you laugh from deep in your belly and out of your fresh-tooth smile. Your happiness is a superpower, pulling people around you to smile and laugh with you.

    I imagine as you grow, you will fall and scrape your knees and elbows learning to walk with the earth beneath your feet. I will scoop you up and hold you close. The safety of my arms and my heartbeat against your ear envelop you in comfort and reassurance.

    The night you left my body, I couldn't understand how someone I envisioned a life with was suddenly no longer there?

    The grief overwhelmed me. It controlled my every move, and the painful longing to hold you, trace my fingers along your perfect skin, and feel your chest rise and fall with your breath was too much. I longed to see you smile and hear you laugh.

Haylee Guiver

The magnitude of feeling I failed to keep you safe crushed me like a fallen concrete wall.

Once the grief subsided, I picked myself up from the depths of sadness and began gently wading through the shallows. The heaviness in my heart slowly eased, and forgiving myself and my body began.

My beautiful daughter, I could begin to feel you.

I feel you when I'm alone.

I feel you when I'm holding your brothers close.

I feel you when I'm happy,

and I feel you when I'm sad.

It was hard. It was really fucking hard feeling you so close but not being able to hold you.

Once that concrete wall around my heart started to crumble, I heard the lesson you were brought to provide.

And now you're all around me.

You're in the wind through the trees.

You're in the warmth from the sun.

You're the smell of the first rain.

You're a butterfly circling me when I need reassurance.

You're a light through the darkness and my constant spirit guide.

You were brought to me to spark my fire and shake my core. You're showing me how to follow my life path and ride my life with the same love, safety and reassurance I planned so deeply to show you.

I may not see you, my beautiful daughter, but I can feel you.

Letters to my Daughter

For my Nieces Makayla & Ruby
Rachel Carmichael

For my nieces, Makayla and Ruby, the custodians of my heart and soul.

I hope you always remember how incredibly bright, brave, creative, powerful, kind, empathetic, generous, beautiful and loved you are.

I hope you never wonder about your worth and always feel joy in fulfilling your life's purpose.

I hope you feel courageous in pursuing the things that fuel your soul and that you experience love every day in new and amazing ways. And on days when this feels hard, and there will be those days, I hope this poem reminds you how important your life is.

I will always be your number one supporter, your fiercest advocate and your biggest fan.

You will always be my purpose and my reason why.

Love, Aunty Rach.

> *I may not have birthed you,*
> *but I think I willed you into existence.*
> *I asked the universe to send me a daughter,*
> *a fierce and mighty warrior babe to love, guide, teach*
> *and protect.*
> *Someone to tell my stories and share my secrets.*
> *A tiny spark of my soul replicated in another human,*
> *a piece of me to linger when I am gone.*
> *I asked the universe for a daughter.*
> *Instead, it sent me heartache.*

Rachel Carmichael

It sent me empty cycles and negative tests.
It showered me with promises in the form of hormones and tracking, medical tests and dollars spent.
And it watched as promises were broken with my heart and my spirit again and again.
I pleaded with the universe to send me a daughter.
I offered up sacrifices and bargained with the devil.
And I cried a thousand body-shaking tears when I knew the time had passed.
I had wanted a daughter, and yet all along, I had you.
The little women in my life who bulldozed their way in loudly and unapologetically, decimating the life I knew and creating a path for the truest and most unwavering love I would ever know
The tiny humans who may not share my name, my house or even my DNA, but with whom I share a bond deeper than oceans and stronger than stone.
And as I look at you and watch you grow,
miniature versions of my sister and me,
I can see that tiny spark of me living on in you.
When you ask a million questions, because the world is full of answers, and you want to know them all at once.
When you laugh, almost hysterically, and no one else is in on the joke.
When you hug me for a few seconds longer when I'm sad, only we know you felt what I was feeling.
When you can't be found without a crystal or a feather or a flower in your hand.
When you dance around the house, sometimes naked, because you're just so damn happy,
I sit, smile, and realise I asked the universe for a daughter,
and instead, it gave me two.

Letters to my Daughter

Love Always and Forever

Sarah Montgomery

Dear Sarah,

I am writing to you today to let you know that it's OK.

You will be OK.

There are beautiful people in this world, and I hope you experience this for yourself.

You can do anything you put your mind to.

You can be anything you want to be. You just have to have a little trust in yourself.

You are Unique. Always remember to love yourself.

It doesn't matter what happens to you, but it does matter what you do about it.

If you feel like things are too hard or you feel like life just sucks, ask the people that love and care for you for help.

Asking for help is strength.

The truly important people in your life will come into your life and never leave.

People will come and go, always treat the people around you well.

Talk to someone about your problems; it will nearly always help.

Try everything once and stand up for what you believe in, even if you are standing alone.

Fall in love, and don't be afraid.

Face everything in life that scares you. It will be empowering, enlightening and good for your soul.

Sarah Montgomery

If you make mistakes, be sure to admit them.
Accept that you may hurt people. The key is to learn from your mistakes.
If you hurt someone, say sorry and show them you won't hurt them again.
If you fail, pick yourself up, dust yourself off and give it another go.
Honesty is the best policy. The truth will always prevail.
Follow your Heart.
Follow your Dreams.
Have goals.
Be True to Yourself.
Never give up on anything that truly sets your soul on fire.
I'm so glad I am aware now, aware of myself, and aware that I didn't know how to deal with a lot of life at a young age.
I'm glad I've been given a chance at true love, which I have found finally.
I'm doing a good job of messing it up and also a good job of learning how to be loved.
Let me tell you, it's really hard to let love in after turning my heart off at a very young age without even realising it.
I understand now why my mum did what she did as a parent.
I misunderstood a lot and refused to hear. It was so different to how I'd become accustomed. Tough!
In saying that, I am a motivated, brave, passionate, direct, random, beautiful and loving young woman.
I am grateful I had people to take care of me every step of the way.
I took that for granted for a long time.
Quite simply, don't do that.
Appreciate what you have at all times.
Love without Fear.
Give without expecting in return.
Laugh a lot.
Cry, but cry from the heart.
Love the skin you're in because we are all flawed and fabulous.
Jealousy is a curse.
Mind your own business.
Find a man or woman who will treat you like the most beautiful princess ever.

Letters to my Daughter

They are out there. There is one who will show you that no one else matters.
Safe.
Secure.
Adored.
Respected.
Trusts in You.
Encourages You.
Cuddles you when you feel down.
Won't make you cry unless you need to pull your head in.
Looks after you even when you are annoying.
Does the little things that mean the most to you.
Spends time with you and makes time for you.
You talk to each other for hours upon hours, time going unnoticed because you are so engrossed in each other.
Never settle for a person who wants to change you.
The right one will help you grow and create the best version of yourself.
Be kind to yourself and realise money can't make you happy, and neither can possessions.
Great people, true people and moments, are what will take your breath away and inspire you to enjoy every moment.
Do what is right for you and what feels good.
Don't be rude or arrogant.
It will get you nowhere very fast.
Open your mind and be curious about other people's perspectives, beliefs, values and morals.
You don't have to agree, but you need to accept them for who they are.
Sarah, I am sorry I didn't accept you for who you were.
It's OK not to be OK.
It's OK to knock down the walls and be close to genuine, caring people.
This is part of being happy.
Always follow your instinct and intuition.
If you do, you will truly shine.
Apply yourself because knowledge is great.
Most importantly,
love and be loved,
live and let live.

Sarah Montgomery

Your world and those in it are all you need to focus on.
Worry will stop you from being present.
Worry doesn't suit you, Sarah.
Lastly, your thoughts create your reality.
Hugs are the best thing in the world, so give and receive them often.
Long, squeezy hugs that last a minute.
Thank you for hearing me today.
Know that I'm grateful for all you have done for me during our life.
Love always and forever.

Letters to my Daughter

For my Daughter
Hayley French

As I sit down to reflect on life with my daughter, mixed emotions rise. It's the end of her primary years and the beginning of high school. I feel heavy in my heart but optimistic about how the future looks for her.

I look back at her growing up, the laughs, the tears, the evenings spent cuddling and watching movies, the holidays, kissing her cheeks, which is one of my favourite things to do in the world. I love the sound of her voice, the curls in her hair and her blue eyes.

I want her to know that she was my strength and reason to keep going when things were tough. Her being there gave me a reason to get up, a purpose.

I watch her practising self-love in the mirror. To notice five things she likes for every one thing she dislikes. To appreciate her own beauty and act with kindness towards herself and others. To hold her power and not to give it away. To be empowered to kick all her goals and raise others up at the same time.

To smile and laugh. Laugh at herself and not take herself too seriously.

I want her to know that she is always beautiful, even when she doesn't feel her best. She doesn't need to be pretty for everyone else. She is just unapologetically beautiful, no matter what.

I wish for her to enjoy life and cultivate gratitude and positivity, even when life beats her down.

I want her to take a moment to breathe when she's overwhelmed, close her eyes and feel into her body.

I wish for her to see the silver lining in everything. I hope she smiles with her eyes and walks tall, her chin held high. Not to absorb the energy of others when it isn't hers to absorb and to know the difference.

To release her thoughts onto paper, not keep them festering in her mind.

I want her to read, grow and enjoy being the best person she can be. To actively practice being a good, kind person. To collect tools that she can use whenever she needs them and share them with others. I want to teach her the ability to ride her energy and work with it.

When energy is low, I want her to know how to rest and not force more than she is physically able. I want her never to feel bad about having a nap, stopping for a breath or taking a still moment.

When her energy is high, I want her to know she can do anything and prioritise her time. To have good solid boundaries around her and to pick her people wisely.

I want her to always feel gratitude for what she has and for what is to come. I want her to visualise her future in detail and create the life she wants. To know, without doubt, she has all the power inside her to make her dreams come true.

I encourage her to take every opportunity to be kind, help and include others. Always be empathetic to what someone else may be going through and never assume that other people see the world the same way she does. I want her to know that everyone has their own life experiences, journey and filters and for her to know that that is perfectly fine.

My dream for my daughter is to live her life to the fullest, dream big and travel far, experience all of the colours of life, have interesting conversations with random people, read books and try different foods. To take pictures and make memories.

I never want her to feel not worthy, not good enough or ugly. I want her to look in the mirror and feel proud of the reflection that looks back at her. I want her to have the confidence just to be her and walk into a room and take up space. To speak her truth and live by her values.

This letter is for all the girls out there, but firstly for my daughter, Layla. It's also for my teenage self and any girl or woman who needs empowerment.

Letters to my Daughter

I Wished for You

Laura Elizabeth

Dear Freyja,

I wished for you. A little girl to dress up and bake with. A little girl to choreograph dances with. A daughter to snuggle with and talk about all the important things going on in your world. I hope I have the right advice to help you navigate life with your heart.

You've always shown so much care and nurturing from an early age. At just two years old, when your little brother was in my belly, I remember I was feeling quite sick. Next thing you know, you appeared with your favourite-cuddly blanket and wrapped it around me as you sang a song and softly patted me with reassurance.

Each year, your teachers mention what a kind, helpful and compassionate friend you are to your peers. This is because you always volunteer to help others with their work or put your hand up to be the teacher's assistant.

I see you always thinking of others and how you can make their day a little brighter by helping them to feel loved, seen and appreciated.

There is always so much joy in your beautiful-big brown eyes when you're relaying a story or telling a joke, and I admire how committed you are to maintaining the perfect bend back and splits. You definitely didn't inherit your flexibility from me.

You have cultivated some seriously delicious baking skills, and I love tasting the treats you so lovingly create to share with your brothers and me and sometimes even Grandad!

Darling girl, you make me proud every single day just by being you. I want you to know that even when things don't work out the way you

Laura Elizabeth

expect, and even if there's a day you feel disappointed, you're still the shining star in my world, making me proud and grateful that you chose me as your mum.

If there's anything I can offer you, my girl, it's that you are loved simply because you are here, and you matter simply because you exist.

Remember that you are worthy of putting yourself first. So, push to the front of the queue, take the last cookie, interrupt conversations with the things that light you up and let your voice be heard.

My advice for you as you grow, and for all the daughters is this...I want you to feel worthy of being seen and heard. I want you to share the joy and dancing that flows from your heart. I want you to keep seeing all the magic in the world.

Please try not to censor yourself or become smaller to fit in, my love.

You are here to inspire magic in the hearts and souls of all who cross your path.

Thank you, thank you, thank you!

I love you to the moon and back, your Mumma.

Letters to my Daughter

A Mother's Gratitude

Janice Cooper

Dear Laura,

I remember a time when all I wanted was to be a mother. So much so that I chose to focus on motherhood rather than pursuing a career like many of my friends were doing. I lacked self-confidence for much of my young life, and the thought of further education, more exams, and perhaps failure were fears I couldn't tolerate.

I had a boyfriend, and we were happy together. We were engaged for two years before marrying two weeks before my nineteenth birthday. The overwhelming desire to become a mother grew stronger, and you came into my life on 12 February 1987, fulfilling my dream and making me a 'mummy' for the first time.

From the moment I saw you, my perception of life changed. I had actually done something meaningful in my life! What I didn't expect was the familiar feeling of fear rising that day when we were transferred from the birthing suite to the labour ward, and I was alone with you.

I was extremely aware of the anxiety I'd felt throughout my school years. Yes, I had succeeded in giving birth to this absolutely perfect little human, but what if I was a failure as a mother?

I had so many questions going through my head. All my doubts and fears were rising. I couldn't fail at this! I was responsible for a tiny-vulnerable little girl who chose me as her mum. I had to step out of my comfort zone and gather all the emotional strength I had to raise a confident, well-adjusted little girl who would one day grow into a much more confident woman than I was.

Janice Cooper

As the years went by, it was clear to see that you were your own person. You met all your childhood goals early, and I think it's fair to say that you were a very challenging toddler at times! I was teaching and influencing the most beautiful-humorous feisty little lady! Even at preschool age, you were happy to throw in the odd expletive when you felt it necessary.

You always seemed aware of situations and were able to read people from a young age. You taught me how to trust my gut instinct more than I had previously done, which is something I still rely on to this day when a difficult decision arises.

You breezed effortlessly through primary school, and I was always proud of the fact that you would join in all sorts of different activities with an ease I'd never experienced at school. I had such a fear of failing that I wouldn't join groups or clubs, and it definitely held me back.

We moved to Perth, Australia, when you were 12-years-old and you began your high school education. How you navigated this enormous lifestyle change was inspiring! Again you taught me ways to fit in with a new workplace, new friends, and a new life. By observing you and the way you trusted your instincts, I too settled into life in Australia.

Throughout your adolescent years, you became the most important female influence in my life. You have taught me that sometimes it's ok to make unbelievably hard choices to enable self-growth and self-love.

An example of this would be the breakdown of your marriage in 2016. This was an emotionally difficult time for our family, and again I was drawn into the fear. How would you cope? Where would you live? What about my precious Grandchildren? But again, you showed resilience and determination, and you have created a stable and loving environment for your children.

The guidance you give them is priceless.

Finally, in November 2019, you invited me to a *Weaving Ancestral Wisdom* workshop that you were facilitating. Though I was unsure, I trusted your judgement and attended. The love in the room for you that day was palpable, and it was clear to see that this was the result of all the sacrifices you'd made to this point. I saw you work at your absolute best, free from the constraints and commitments of marriage, helping all those beautiful women. I have nothing but pride in the work you do, the passion you have, and the honest-beautiful person you are.

Letters to my Daughter

You have helped me in more ways than you know, and for that, I thank you.

I am so grateful to be able to put pen to paper here and tell you what an amazing daughter you are!

Laura Elizabeth, I thank you for choosing ME x

Your Birth and Chocolate

Nellie Barnett

The other day, my love, I asked you the question, 'If I died, what would you like to read about in a written piece of legacy left from me to you?'

'Chocolate,' you replied, with an ever-growing cheeky glint in your eye. 'Nah', you went on, 'let me think about it.'

Later, you returned and stood before me declaring, 'Birth. My birth. That's what I want you to write about.'

And so this is, my love, a letter to you, my daughter, about your birth… and chocolate.

You came into this world, my love, much like you do life, head first, head-strong and on your own terms. It's been one of my biggest parenting challenges so far, your attitude, because God knows the world needs that kind of rebellion and conviction right now. I don't want to separate you from that or dim it, but can you please just clean your freaking room?

It was 4.15 am on a Thursday dawning when I knew I would be meeting you very soon.

The *'pop'* of your magic-womb bubble bursting signalled the start of your journey Earthside and the separating of us as one body, into two, physically. But the truth is that as a mother, I can never truly consider myself separate from you, not completely. Part of me in you and you in me will ALWAYS remain. It's one of those precious and heart-wrenching things that comes with growing a life inside of you. So, if you ever feel emotionally or physically far away from me, you can read this letter and remember that we are always a part of each other.

Your birth took over my body.

Letters to my Daughter

It started slow, then came on fast. We were at home, in our beautiful little cottage by the sea, where I felt safe and comfortable. We'd planned a water birth for you to flow into this world through, but you had other ideas! Your heart was set on the big-red couch, it seemed, and I knew quite quickly that the pool filling evvveerrrr sooooo slooowwlllly just wasn't going to be where I'd get to meet you.

For the first two hours, I wondered when I'd feel anything more.

Then a few little ripples of your becoming started to stir in my belly, my womb.

At the three-hour mark, I was strongly questioning my choice to give birth at home, without drugs or intervention, as each contraction, each movement of you towards your first breath, completely rocked me. *If I've got many hours of this, I've made a huge mistake,* I thought. A moment of doubt. But the body kept doing what it's so divinely designed to do, and you were stopping for no one. You were definitely my daughter.

At four hours, it was clear you were coming, and fast.

Just like your conception, the essence of you was there from the beginning.

'Look out world; I'm coming. Against all the odds, and no, you don't really have much of a say in it.'

This is the first thing I ever heard you say, in my heart, when you landed in my womb. I loved you immediately for all that you were and signed over my body for the required period in a contract written, I suspect, in star-ink many, many lifetimes ago.

Yours was an intensely physiological and involuntary style of labour, very different to your brother's more recently. I never really felt like I had to think about what to do next or make it happen, no trying to push, no what do I need to do to help this progress? Your birth literally happened by itself, with my body and my breath simply supporting the process intuitively, instinctively, innately.

Even our midwife was surprised when I declared calmly, 'I think I need to push!'

'Really?' she replied.

But a quick look confirmed that the body knew best.

And so, you came, within a few pushes and within four and a half hours, onto the big red couch matching your little red face, screaming your way into the world with the declaration that you'd arrived.

Nellie Barnett

You were healthy and perfect and mind-blowingly real.

The birthing pool was ready for us then, and so we slipped in together, easing into the warm water like a big-silky hug.

I went from just a girl to your mum in an instant.

Forever changed.

Forever grateful that you chose me to experience life through.

And chocolate, where does chocolate come into the story, you might wonder?

Nutella.

It comes in the form of Nutella—the first thing I ate after you were born.

Toast with Nutella topped with strawberries and bananas.

It was divine. Just like you, my daughter…sweet and rich and delicious and loved by so many and just a little bit nutty and the perfect amount of ever-so-slightly naughty in all the best ways.

I love you to the moon and back, my daughter, and an infinite amount of time, space and distance more.

Thank you for choosing me and making me a Mother.

Love, Mama Nellie.

Letters to my Daughter

My Eternal Love

Briony J

Dear Lara—born sleeping,

You were born at 4.52 pm, but it was already too late.

Resuscitation and a shot of adrenalin into your tiny heart started it beating. You tried your best to take a breath so you could say hello, but this was not to be as you quickly had to go.

How is a mother meant to say goodbye to their child is a question I never thought I would ask. As I held you for the very last time, I tried my hardest to burn you into my memory so I could recall every perfection of your beauty forever.

I demanded time to stop. I never wanted to let you go, but I handed you over and cried out, 'I love you', as the nurse walked out the door, and my baby was gone forever.

That day in December, my world changed instantly, and a part of me died with you. I blamed myself for you leaving too soon. I wondered if I had done more or gone to the hospital earlier, if the outcome may have been different, but there is only so long I can play that game over in my head.

I still cry for you when no one is watching. Time does not heal all wounds, but it lessens the pain.

I treasure the moments I felt you in the many months we were as one, Mother and Daughter. It's a closeness no one else could share.

I shall never see you grow into the woman I knew you would be.

You will never hear me whisper, 'I love you', as I hug you tight.

Nor will you feel the touch of my gentle kiss as you rest your head at night.

Briony J

I have transformed my suffering into learning and my heartache into resilience, and for that, I thank you.

Your legacy to the world was introducing me to the true meaning of love and loss and gave me the ability to share this with others I meet working on the frontlines.

I have reached out my hand to console strangers in their time of need and have been able to say I understand their loss wholeheartedly. For a fleeting moment, when they look into my eyes, they see the truth and recognise there is hope on the other side of pain, and for this, I am eternally grateful.

They say all children go to heaven, so as you sit there watching over us, know that having you was an unimaginable blessing, and my worst experience has become my most profound learning.

Until I hold you again,
Mum xx

Dear AJ,

Before you were born, you were a fighter. A rare heart condition was never going to hold you back. The nurses took you from me to ICU, and I fought to see you so I could kiss you goodbye, not knowing if this would be goodbye forever again. My ultimate job as a mother is to protect you, but I was scared I would fail once more, and I built walls to shield myself. It took time for me to trust you were not going to leave me like your sister, and for that, I apologise.

As your mother, I promise to do my best and show you the way to independence. Being a woman is an amazing gift, but it also comes with some challenges; not everything is equal even now. Therefore, never grow out of questioning the why. Refuse to conform to outdated expectations and stay true to your gentle soul. For an unbound spirit, the world is a wonderful place to create your mark, and it awaits more passionate women to make a difference.

Although you may not always take my advice, as the years' age, you may one day fall back on this:

Choose to go beyond.
It's always too soon to quit.
Don't be scared to take opportunities.
Live your life your way.

Letters to my Daughter

Put justice and kindness before all else.

Your blood runs thick with a history of strong women, and my dear, you are no different. Being your mother and watching you grow has been my greatest honour. You are a voice for the quiet, a protector of the vulnerable and a guardian of the fragile, and I want you to share your precious gift with the waiting world. And as you move through life, I can't promise many things, but I can promise life won't always be easy. So when those days come, I want you to remember:

You are the reason I kept going,

You are strong and intelligent,

Don't chase perfection because you are beautiful and amazing the way you are,

You are, and will always, be enough,

You will forever have my eternal love and unconditional support.

I love you. Mum xx

Alysha Christensen

To my Darling Katelyn

Alysha Christensen

To my darling Katelyn or Kate-Kate, as your big brother calls you,

We didn't find out the gender when I was pregnant, but your dad wanted a daughter. He wanted the opportunity to walk her down the aisle on her wedding day. He's an amazing Dad. You are so lucky, my darling. We both are.

When do I begin? I have a daughter.

What a beautifully terrifying gift. As I write this, you're seven months old. Time is moving too fast. I close my eyes and see you twirling and giggling around the living room. I can see you going to school. I'm not ready for that.

How do I keep you safe? My beautiful girl. The world can be so cruel. I hope with every cell in my body that life treats you well.

That strong, passionate, warm-hearted souls surround you.

My mind focuses on you in high school because, my love, that's where it gets tough. I ache to protect you, prepare you, and fiercely defend you against anybody who means you harm. I have no idea what the world will look like for you as a teenager. Heck, I don't even know what the world will look like for us next year, and that's just weeks away.

Can I let you in on a secret? If you're reading this, which I will obviously force upon you the moment you can understand it (#proud), growing up isn't all that great.

Did you just roll your eyes?

You probably did.

'But Mum, I can't WAIT to grow up.'

Trust me, my darling, you absolutely can! I know, that's such a grown-up thing to say. I get it.

Letters to my Daughter

Man, do I wish I could be a kid again. But since I can't, here's what I've learnt and what I hope I do a good job passing on to you.

Sometimes you're going to feel like nobody gets it. There will be times you feel scared, nervous, and awkward as hell. There will be boys when mummy and daddy let you start dating at twenty-one. Some will probably break your heart. Girls will be mean, and friends will come and go. You'll probably hate everybody for a minute.

But that's okay.

It's all going to be okay. It's growth and growth is messy. You are transforming into an adult.

I wonder what she will be like? I hope she still adores her mum. Are we best friends? Probably.

There is light all around you, my gorgeous girl. You just have to look for it. Look for it in people, animals, and how the breeze moves the trees around you.

If there's one time to listen to your mum, it's now.

It's okay to sit in your feelings and to feel all of them. If you need to cry, then cry. Laugh, dance, scream if you need to. Honour your feelings. They are valid and YOU, my sweet daughter, are valid.

You are important.

You are beautiful. And I know this because I made you, and I'm very good at making things.

Growing up is a roller coaster. I hope your dad and I hold you through it in a way that makes you feel seen, safe and loved. Because you are so, so loved.

You will find your people. You will have good days and bad days. You'll learn to drive and spend your days at the beach with friends. You'll probably get sunburnt, and we'll lecture you when you get home.

You'll worry about your looks. This one scares me the most. Will your dad and I do enough to make sure you know just how beautiful you are? Will we teach you that beauty is about what's inside? Will we teach you kindness and compassion? Will watching your dad and me show you what love is? Will you know how a woman deserves to be treated by watching how your dad loves your mum? Will you settle for nothing less than what you've grown up seeing?

Love. Friendship. Respect.

I want so much for you, my beautiful girl. It terrifies me to raise a daughter.

Alysha Christensen

I don't feel qualified. But, we live in a time where the power of women is starting to get louder. It's beautiful.

Women are CEOs. Mums are killing it at mum life, which for the record, is HARD. It's the hardest but most rewarding job there is. They're dreaming up businesses and turning them into million-dollar companies.

They're claiming their power.

I hope we see this tenfold in your lifetime. I want you to know how truly powerful you are, my girl. I want you to know that whatever you dream of, you can do. You have no idea how capable you are. Find other women who inspire you, who are out chasing their dream life.

People will doubt you, judge you, and not believe in you. Ignore them. Ignore them until you're so in love with your life that you don't even notice them.

Life is short. You will grow up, I promise. But for now, please enjoy being young. Enjoy those days at the beach, the times at the mall stalking the cute boys. Enjoy it all because you'll be that grown-up you ache to be before long.

I can wait to meet her. I'm not ready yet. For now, I'm going to go and cuddle you as you drift off to sleep on my chest while I sing *Twinkle Twinkle* softly into your ear. I will smell your hair and kiss your cheek as you snore into my neck.

I love you so, so much, Katelyn. One day, if you're lucky enough to be a Mum, you'll know just how deep that love is. A mother's love for her child is beyond what I can describe.

Chase your dreams, beautiful girl.

Love your biggest fan, Mum.

Letters to my Daughter

Poems for my Daughter
Nicole Aly

Oceans

You were born from a wound
Somehow you knew
That you would be different
You would be you

Angelic and sweet
Content to just be
You found your sound
Firmly planted in the ground

In touch with your body
You move carefree
Unafraid of your quirks
You sing of big butts
As you bust out a twerk

The love inside you
Grows by the day
My heart swells with adoration
You're magnificence at play

Nicole Aly

Beware of the burdens
Some are too heavy
Not yours to shoulder
Be discerning as you get older

Take time to breathe, live in the moment
Question fairytales and unicorn involvement
Run with your cats, you're wild, and you're free
It's your life to live, unapologetically

As the sun sets
We catch another wave
Remember your worth
Is as infinite as the ocean we crave.

I love you.

Always Enough

Generations of scars
Wounds I inherit
Entombed in our suffering
Whispers we parrot

Generational trauma
Bound in shame
The same security and blame
Repeated again and again

Your voice is not yours
It's not safe to be wild
Your value is cheap
Don't speak, dear child

Wrapped in a bow
Pretty and neat

Letters to my Daughter

Worn on the outside
A possession to keep

Acceptance of self
Forgiveness of mother
Look to the mirror
Not the eyes of another

The thickness of thighs
The curve of my hips
The eyes of my soul
The words from my lips

My softness
My round
My firm
My edges

The womb of creation
The beat of my drum
The magic I weave
The sorrow undone

My soul is exposed
My essence is free
My worth is my own
My voice is me

With all my Love

Trish Bond

As you are almost an adult, I wanted to write this letter to share these things with you. I hope you will read it whenever you feel like you need it.

I can't put into words how much joy and happiness you've bought into my life. I feel your joy and your pain. There have been times when I've struggled to get up and move, times that I thought it was too hard to carry on. I feel so much love for you, and that's what's kept me going when the load is almost too hard to bear. Thank you for blessing me with having you in my life. You inspire me to be better and achieve things that I perhaps would not have done without you.

During my life, there were times when I felt alone, and I had to struggle through on my own. I often wished I had a mother who I could talk with and who could share my fears and doubts. I wish I had received guidance to spare me some of the hard lessons I have learned. However, that was not my journey. I am grateful that I am here for you and hope you never have to experience that.

Please know that I am here for you when you need me. If I am busy or distracted, you just need to get my attention and help me realise that you need my ear, shoulder, support or guidance. This is your journey, and I hope you find the happiness you deserve and find where you fit in the world and are accepted just as you are. I know you will make a positive difference in the world.

There is nothing that will stop me from loving you. No matter how bad you feel it is. I will love you forever and ever, no matter what.

Letters to my Daughter

You have so much potential to make a difference to those around you. You are a kind, caring and beautiful soul. You deserve to have everything good in your life.

I would like to share some words of wisdom with you. I hope that some of them will resonate. Some may resonate now and others later. Take what you wish and apply them to your life if it feels right for you.

You don't have to be the best. You just have to do your best.

Become the best version of yourself that you possibly can.

Listen to your heart. Feel with your heart. Your heart and passion will guide you in the right direction if you let it.

You don't have to be like anyone else because you are you, and you are unique.

Sometimes we can be our own worst critics. Perhaps you could choose to be your own best friend instead. Simply apply the advice you would give your best friend to yourself. Be kind to yourself instead of having such high expectations of yourself.

Throughout your life, there will be things that happen outside your control. That is ok. Things happen for a reason, and sometimes we may not understand that reason for a long time, or not at all.

Take the lesson and remove the emotion. The emotion is there to help you understand the lesson.

Don't compare yourself to anyone else. Everyone's journey is different.

Find your tribe, your people. When you find them, you will know it because people will accept you for who you are.

Listen to your intuition. Your feelings are there to help guide you throughout your life. Sometimes those feelings will be subtle but try not to dismiss them.

If you need help, then please ask for it. No matter how trivial it may seem, there will always be someone willing to listen. If you can't find someone physically to connect with, perhaps try spirit through prayer or ask an angel, your guides or loved ones.

You are stronger than you think.

Face your fear, and find acceptance of that fear, and then you will find your freedom.

I believe in you.

Please always remember—I love you, no matter what.

Trish Bond

Finally, I would like to tell you that you are loved more than you could possibly know.
With all my love,
Mum.

Letters to my Daughter

Daughters of the World

Chantelle Dawn Skye

Dear Daughters of the World,
    Breathe.
    Breathe deep into your belly.
    Breathe deep into your heart.
    Breathe deep into your womb.
    Close your eyes and listen. Listen to your own inner wisdom. What does she want to say?
    It is time for you to bear witness to the divinity within yourself. Time for you to know the person hiding beneath the bullshit fed to you by this world. The bullshit that keeps you small. Breaking free from the person they tell you to be is fucking scary, but it is time. Let them fear you but do not fear yourself.
    Your emotions fuel you. Feel them. They are your superpower. Feel all of your big feelings. Cry. Scream. Roar. Let them hear your voice. Allow your voice of truth to reverberate out into this world and let them know that you are stepping into your power. Let them hear you because you are here to set this world on fire with the words that sing through you.
    Be misunderstood. Be crazy. Live a life that others don't quite get. It is this in-between world where you will have the opportunity to meet the delicate soul that is you. Be nude. See yourself within the naked truth of who you are. Teach others that they do not need to understand you to respect you, to hear you or see you. Let them know you because you do not care what they think of you.
    Love big, love loud and love hard. Just know that many will desire

you, but only a rare few will desire to claim you. So yes, you bleed for this world, and you will also bleed your love into others who do not wish to hold you in the way you deserve. Do not allow those who only desire what your body can provide dare tell you what you are worth. If you do descend into this shadow world, let it be brief and know that your rise will be spectacular. Let them have you but know your worth.

There are those in this world that will demand you give in, give up and hand over your light so they may take what is not theirs to take. Honour your desires, be sensual, hear your primal heartbeat, and dance to your own soul song. Tease and tantalise, arouse your own pleasure.

Be provocative, but learn where your boundaries lie within your body and my darlings, only consent to your full-body fuck yes! Let them feel you because you are a goddess.

Daughters, I implore you to be brave. Be fierce. Invoke the Divine Feminine that resides beneath your skin and seek for what it is she longs for in this world. Be kind, and please be gentle with yourself. Forgive yourself for your mistakes. This life is a path we all walk, and none of us will ever get it one hundred per cent right. Plant your feet on Mother Earth and take up space. Crave for that which is you to ignite the wildfire within and set your world alight.

You do not need to be perfect. You just need to be you. So when the fear and doubt take hold…

Breathe.
Breathe deeply into your belly.
Breathe deeply into your heart.
Breathe deeply into your womb.
Close your eyes and listen. Hear your own deep innate wisdom.
You are your own magic.

Birth of A Queen

I am invoking my power to love this Queen
Enjoying seeing all that was unseen
and feeling all that has been unfelt because it is okay to
have feelings

Letters to my Daughter

I am not broken, but I am fucking healing
I have walked the trail of a wasteland
Which led me to the intricacies of my soul
Like the sun's fingers playing with the sky, I am heavenly and whole
I am moonlight and daydreams, sensual divinity and a flirt
To be made of magic and not believe it
This is the hurt
Into the wild unknown, I go
Never to be bound and tame
Gently breathing her open
She is birthed from the Great Mother's wame
I hear the call that is surging for her to rise
To trust how deep this is going
Finally, I am at ease within my own inherent knowing
Within this power I own, I am the Fuckening
Prepare yourself to embrace
When you are ready, I am here for you
I'll hold the loving space
So you can feel all that has been unfelt because it is okay to have feelings
Queens, we are not broken, but we are fucking healing

More than all the Moon and Stars

Dawn Mills

'I'm ready,' I said, climbing onto the bed.

Within minutes you passed through my legs and into my hands.

My first thoughts were how hot you were, like a fresh loaf out of the oven. Your face is a little battered and bruised with swollen eyes from catching your face on the way out. At that moment, I knew what a tough-little cookie I was blessed with for my second born. No big cry, just the gentle sound of your first breath and I marvelled at how quickly you arrived. Vernix covered you and was caked in your beautiful head of thick-dark hair.

My quiet, clingy mama's girl, who loved the boob, refused to eat from a spoon and struggled to let me out of her sight for the longest time. Now we all laugh and accept you're still a fussy eater unless nachos are on the menu. Sweet-stubborn cherub who sticks to her guns, knows her own mind and stands by her choices. Your brother's shadow, often mistaken for twins when we went out, mirroring his actions and copying his movements. The love shone from your face like moonbeams whenever you looked at him. My little-brown bomber, tanned from outdoor play, throwing yourself fearlessly into the pool and swimming like a little fish.

I am proud and inspired by how you walk in this life, unafraid to be who you are, embracing all sides of yourself and living a full and rich life. My girl, who pursues her dreams, throws herself off cliff tops to dive into the ocean. So brave. I'm floored by your strength, especially when things tumble out of your control. Fear is acknowledged, but you push through, surprising me with how fearless you are as you build a beautiful life.

Letters to my Daughter

Thank you for choosing me, my treasure. I get to enjoy the gold.

Baby number three arrived on a calm and quiet morning—a strange feeling in the air. To our delight, a pair of ducks chose that day to land in our pool for a paddle. We arrived at the birthing centre, and within an hour, you were born. There was no time for the midwife to fit her gloves properly, and just like your sister, you were passed into my hands on the floor of the shower. It felt primal to cut your cord. It is a moment forever etched in my mind as one of my finest. I was elated!

Born at lunchtime, our little family bonded, and Manya was so happy to be surrounded by her three grandies. Then it was just us. We fed, napped, and I ached to take you home. By dinnertime, we were at the neighbours, and I delighted in showing you off. For two weeks, I was on high, loving life and relishing being a Mum for the third time around. And then the call came that turned our world upside down. Your Aunty Paula passed away, and with this news, I was swept away by waves of grief that changed me forever.

For six months or more, I was on autopilot, and sadly I don't remember much as I struggled to find my place in this world. Guilt-ridden and unable to enjoy everything my only sister would never know. How I wish to gain that lost time over, please forgive me.

How blessed I am to have such a beautiful, thoughtful mini-me. The one who loves to bring the family together and treats friends like family with the same thought and care. I adore how we share the same humour. Naughty girl, you absolutely delight me. It's so thoughtful how you care for me, share your friendships, and include me in your life. How I love when you ask for sleepovers and the absolute joy I feel because now I ask you. Our kisses, lips to lips, are priceless, my love. You once asked me if it's weird? Never. As we say, 'Love you, love you more.'

It's inspiring when I reflect on how committed you are to your work, finding joy in connections and giving service to others. I see you and cheer for you. I'm forever there for you, and you are forever there for me. We know this is our truth. Never doubt your wonderful self. You bring sunshine and joy, and I am excited about what lies ahead for you. I'm so proud of the life you are paving. Embrace your fine self, take every day as it comes, celebrate life, and enjoy what's in store.

To my three cherubs, I love you more than all the moon and stars xx.

My Little Firecrackers

Ashlea Carpenter

I never wanted to get married. I didn't want kids either.

I actually envisioned myself as a single parent of a child I never planned for. It's funny how things turned out so differently.

When I was twenty, a friend asked me to do a pregnancy test with her because she was late and worried. As it turned out, I was the one who displayed those two pink lines. The universe loved to test me and teach me lessons.

I was almost through my first trimester; I had one week to make a choice. We took precautions! How did I not see the signs? I was terrified. I didn't want my parents to know because I feared they would be infuriated. I kept it a secret for three days before I broke down and told my mum. I begged her not to tell my dad. She told him anyway. I was shocked when they explained that they weren't angry and would support me no matter my decision. I honestly expected them to blow up at me, and I'm grateful they understood.

I knew what I needed to do, and that was to choose what was right for me at that moment. Shit, I couldn't look after myself, let alone another life. It wasn't fair on the child. It wasn't fair on my partner, and our relationship was anything but stable.

So I made the controversial decision against what I believed and sent my future on a different trajectory.

I sat in the waiting room amongst other women making the same decision. To say it was difficult is an understatement. The constant argument between my head and my heart hurt beyond comprehension.

Letters to my Daughter

They wheeled me in, and the heavy doors behind me closed.

Fast forward twelve years, and here we are.

I'm still in disbelief that I created two beautiful souls. I'm still trying to figure it all out. Every day seems so surreal. Ask any mother, and they'll tell you that from the very second you discover that you're pregnant, everything changes, and you would move the heavens and earth for a child you haven't even met yet. You'll do anything to protect them, and you'll cherish every moment with them, no matter how stressed or exhausted you are.

Now that I am older, I've realised that I want to teach you all I wish I'd learnt.

I've had best friends betray me.

I've had family members allow their incarcerated lovers to threaten me.

I've failed to set boundaries, and I've bitten my tongue to keep the peace.

I've been lied to and cheated on more times than I can count.

I've felt guilty every time I said no.

I've ignored my instincts.

I've both lost and found myself many times.

I've had my private thoughts read aloud and scolded for what I'd written.

I've lost friends way before their time.

I've had my parents separate after almost thirty years.

I've helped my dad through grief, from both loss and love.

I've helped my mum escape her abuser.

I've let people tell me who I am or should be.

You set the standard of how people treat you. Make sure you set it immediately.

Some of these things should have broken me; however, I'm not going to be a victim.

My past sounds worse than it was. I could never say I lived a tough life, but I've lived through some tough times.

I wouldn't change a single thing because everything brought me to you.

I could tell you how much I love you, how you make each day brighter and how your laughter is my favourite sound, but if I've done my job right, you should already know all of this. What I do want to tell you, though, is that not every day will be sunshine and rainbows. It's what you make of this life that means the most. Don't allow anyone to

Ashlea Carpenter

tell you that you aren't enough. You are so much more. When I look into your bright blue eyes, I see infinite possibilities. I see a spark that no one can extinguish.

I'm looking forward to learning all about you and how you will break the generational curse and kick-arse. You will move mountains, and I can't wait to get caught in your storm.

My little firecrackers, I know that you're going to set this world on fire.

Letters to my Daughter

My Precious Child

Fiona Dyer

To my precious child,

I'm writing this letter to share some of my wisdom with you.

Life doesn't come with a rule book because it's yours to create!

If there is one gift that I want you to have above all others, it's the gift of intuition and trusting yourself. That deep inner voice will keep you safe and guide you well.

Even though you saw my heartbreak, I want you to love with your whole heart. I know it's hard sometimes, and the world can knock you down but know that you have the power to get up and try again, just like when you were a baby learning to walk. You fell down many times. It was frustrating and seemed hard, and you probably thought you'd never get there but look at you now!

Your mind is so powerful. It's important to learn how to harness it. Learn to love and adore yourself. I know this can be a challenge but start by focusing on doing what you love and bringing yourself joy. For example, what movies, music, and hobbies make you feel most like yourself? Know them and hold onto them throughout your relationships, life's challenges and parenthood. Hold onto the things that make you the magical person you are. Create time for yourself, don't give it all away to others. Don't allow the opinions of others about things you love make you shrink or stop doing them.

Have boundaries. Boundaries teach people how to treat us. It's OK to say no! Actually, it's really important learning how to say no. By knowing yourself deeply and well, you'll know what doesn't feel right for you. Whether choosing what to wear, who you're in a relationship with or how you're treated, you deserve to feel loved, cherished and adored.

Life has many twists and turns but don't be afraid to live it. It's like a Choose Your Own Adventure novel. Change it if you take a path that doesn't work out or you don't like it. Have the courage to start over and start a new path. There are no failings, only learnings.

Have the courage to blaze a path and choose a life that brings you joy. Be YOU, truly you, with all your magical quirks. It will help you find your tribe more quickly.

Learn about yourself. What do you love? What makes you feel happy, sad, angry, passionate and excited? Learn what soothes you when times are tough. Things that aren't destructive like drugs and alcohol but are loving like a walk on the beach, watching your favourite movie, journaling, meditation, or time with loved ones.

Feel your emotions and express yourself. Suppressed emotions lead to disease in the body. Constantly pushing down feelings makes them fester. Find a way to let it out. Some people use exercise, play music, do art or seek therapy. Know when to ask for help. It's not failing if you ask for help. It's just seeking answers and support from an outside source. We all need help from time to time. There is no shame in asking. Find a therapist that makes you feel safe, seen and heard. You'll heal better if you like and trust them.

Rest when you need to rest. Listen to your body and your soul, and do what's best for you.

You matter!
You are amazing!
You are loved!
You deserve to be heard!
You deserve to be treated with love, kindness and compassion!
You are so loved, so incredibly wanted, cherished and adored.
I'm so proud of you and all you are each day because you are YOU!
Lots of love,
Mum xxx.

Letters to my Daughter

Unborn

Lauren Maglin

I wake from dreaming of you and sit on the edge of the bed. Tears well in my eyes and spill down my cheeks. My heart aches. I hold my womb as the river flows, and I bleed.

I wonder how different my life would be if I had conceived you, carried you and felt each movement and kick, watching my breasts and belly swell. What would it have been like to birth you? To sit in wonderment at your tiny hands and rock you in my arms with each cry. What would it feel like to have you suckle my breast, nurse you, and sing love songs I had written just for you, my child, while you lay on my chest?

I imagine I smell the fragrance of your skin and twist soft-curly locks around my fingers. You coo, we giggle and laugh. This joy, this fullness that overflows my being, my daughter, my beauty, how I wanted you so, I'm so happy you are here.

I look into your eyes, and I love you completely. I love all the places in you that others did not love in me. I love all the places in you that I could not love in myself until I looked upon your face and saw the truth of beautiful innocence—the truth of real love. You are so safe. I am here with you always.

If ever there was a yearning or an emptiness inside you, know right now that I am holding your hand and sitting with you. I understand your ache and in-completeness as a motherless child to the childless mother. With each year that passed when I dreamed of you, you never came, my womb left unused, I lamented in the echo of your absence all around me in the arms of other women, other families with children playing in the sun. You always seemed out of reach, but I felt I could almost touch you, sweetheart, almost.

Know beloved, that wherever your life takes you, there is no right or wrong way to be a woman. There is your way, and her way is gilded in gold, celebrated in great halls.

You were not born to fit in, don't try to conform to those around you. Instead, in each moment, marvel at your unbridled heart. You belong everywhere, Daughter, inside to out.

Understand you create your belonging every day with each juicy swell or heartbreaking delusion of defeat. No matter the world that may swirl and curl you, scream or whisper to you sweet-beautiful notes or darn dirty lies, believe your truth. You have created the world you live in, and live in it you must. This place is yours to bend, break, mould and flourish in as you see fit. Who you choose to love, how you choose to play, who you decide to fuck, what job you have, if you bear children or don't or can't. Each space and place is an opportunity to refine and stock this divinity that is you. And what a sight to behold as you grow.

As you learn and unlearn, do and re-do, as you sit and do nothing in a field watching the clouds roll over the sky, hair turning silver from gold, your life will be vast. It will be beautiful with people, and it will be beautiful without people. You will always have your heart.

Letters to my Daughter

Made with Love
Fiona Cartledge

My daughters,
　Your heart holds the key to unlocking any door that is meant for you. With patience, courage and belief, you can create the life you've always wanted. Nothing is permanent, and change is inevitable, so hold on and enjoy the ride knowing you are on the path that is destined to be yours. When in doubt, picture, manifest, hope, dream and do the work as if it is already taking place.
　Believe in yourself. Believing in yourself is power.
　Talk to your inner voice as if you were talking or giving advice to your very best friend. Love yourself, no, I mean actually truly, deeply love yourself. It took me until I was in my thirties.
　Look in the mirror, deep into your eyes, the doorways to your soul, and say 'I love you,' say, 'You are amazing,' say, 'I've got you,' and 'I see you,' say, 'Yes you can'.
　My daughters, you are the women of the future. You are made with love. You hold everything you need and want within you. You are already worthy of remarkable things because you are amazing! Like attracts like, and you are love. I'm not an expert on much, but I know love. If someone asked me what's the meaning of life, without hesitation, I'd say love. Love yourself, others and the life you live.
　　Enjoy the little things, like gazing at the sky, night or day. Enjoy the freshness of the air or waves crashing against your legs. Smile back at strangers. Give compliments, say them, express them and be you. Do what makes you happy, what makes your heart smile and your soul dance. Remember how

you feel during these moments because they are the most precious gifts. I'm so lucky I can remember all my favourite moments and feelings watching you enjoy what you are so, so good at, dancing and moving your body.

My eldest daughter, this is for you. You are good at whatever you do, and truly I am so very proud of you. You inspire me and have given me courage. It is because of you that I'm reminded of how very special I am. You are my forever. You will never fail. Life is full of lessons, and you don't need to do it perfectly. Just give it a go. Anything that brings you down, anything negative, flip it, transform it, use it as power and free yourself from any darkness that brings you down. You are light, and you are here to shine bright.

I love you both dearly, and I hope you know how much. All I can say is it's immeasurable. Stand tall, rest when needed, love yourself and back yourself. Treat others well and always know you are perfectly you, and that is so beautiful.

Gratitude

I'd say everything changed dramatically for me in my mindset when I was more grateful. Even when things didn't feel like they were going my way, I'd find something or someone to be grateful for. Happiness doesn't come as a result of getting something but rather recognising and appreciating what we already have or who we already have.

Positivity

With power and positivity, you can turn your pain into your passions, your purpose and even your profession. We all have a story to tell, and the best part of my story is you. Treat your body like it is a temple and only put the best in it. Many of the moments ahead will be creatively disguised as ordinary days, but we all have the chance to make something incredibly magical out of them.

You hold the key to your happiness. Life can be such a wonderful gift

Letters to my Daughter

when you think of how lucky you are to have a ticket to be alive and be on this magnificent journey.

So I hope this letter reminds you that you have gifts within that have never been opened and journeys patiently waiting to be explored. Girls, you have so much going for you, you are so special, and you have futures that are in the best hands. You need to remember this! If you have dreams you have always wanted to come true, you have what it takes to make them happen because you have you! If you ever feel stuck, confused or overwhelmed, surrender to it and ask for guidance.

LOVE ALWAYS MUM, also known as YOUR BIGGEST FAN.

Beautiful Soul

Tanya Morriss

You were born seven weeks early, but you had a fierce spark in your heart from the moment you were earthside. Seeing your perfect little squishy face for the first time was one of the most memorable moments of my life. A strong and beautiful soul that softened the hardened exterior life had formed around me.

When I was young, losing my mother left me with deep heartache and pain. Just thinking of the important moments in my life that she would not be there to experience with me was gut-wrenching and unfathomable.

'Give it time,' people said.

I never really understood how time heals the wound of a heart torn open, left raw and aching with the reality of such a loss.

Memories are such a core part of what creates our whole being. When I was a little girl, I spent every Sunday at my nan's house. My aunty bought buckets of roses and other blooms that I would arrange into vases around the house. This is such a strong and vivid memory that I have held on to my whole life. My passion for flower arranging was formed without even realising it. My nan's house held so many memories: happiness, moments of anger, frustration and confusion, but most of all, laughter and love.

Sometimes we create memories that we don't realise will impact our lives so drastically. This unintentional love for flowers when I was young is what eventually led me to the love of my life, your father, whom I met while working as a florist. Which, in turn, led to you, my little love.

Life has proven to have so many challenges and unexpected turns we cannot foresee or plan for. Existence is not there to be controlled but experienced

Letters to my Daughter

and felt with every emotion pouring into your soul. Surround your being with those that resonate with your heart's intentions. Seek the guidance you will come to crave.

Feel every moment.

Move with the grace and strength you were born with. Take moments to enjoy the journey—the fleeting moments to the toughest. No one is like you. There is only one you, my love.

Make the most of your precious life with the same passion and emotion I felt when you first came into this world—my strong, intelligent and beautiful warrior.

Your existence is a miracle in itself.

My Darling Elodie

Ashleigh Moreland

To my darling daughter, Elodie,

At the time of writing this, you are five years old, and your answer to everything is 'I know'.

'Sweetheart, you are so loved.'

'I know.'

'Darling, you are so smart.'

'I know.'

'You are such a kind person.'

'I know.'

'You are such a great sister.'

'I know.'

'You are an amazing listener.'

'I know.'

'You are such a wonderful friend'.

'I know.'

'You can be anyone you want to be and do anything you want to do.'

'I know.'

When you look 'beflablious' wearing a full-blown party dress covered in sparkles, tights and flamboyant skirt, runners with no socks, and your hair in pigtails you crafted yourself,

I tell you how beautiful you are, and your response is simply, 'I know'.

Nothing fills my heart as much as hearing 'I know' when I tell you how loved you are because, for so much of my life, I believed a lie, that I was unlovable. I felt undeserving. I felt like my worthiness of love was conditional to me acting, looking or thinking a certain way. If I ever made even a minor mistake or didn't achieve some ridiculously high standard, I demonised myself with relentless thoughts that I wasn't good enough to be loved.

I abandoned myself in my quest to please others, so they wouldn't abandon me because even if someone loved me a little bit, it was more than I loved myself. I did this for so many years that I completely lost sight of who I was.

I put the needs of others ahead of my own so that they would love me. I settled for relationships that I knew were dysfunctional and believed I was lucky because someone wanted me and sometimes acted lovingly towards me. I said yes to things that I desperately wanted to say no to so I could please other people. I suppressed my voice when I needed to speak up to keep the peace. I had to be so many versions of me, to so many people, just to feel like I was enough or, even more frequently, not too much. And I don't ever recall my innate response to being told I was loved as being 'I know'.

I am so grateful to have exposed these lies and learned the truth about who I am and what I deserve. Elodie, I am grateful to be your mum for a million different reasons, but especially for the gift of enjoying your childlike innocence. You remind me to laugh more, play more, and be more present.

I am grateful for your unwavering self-confidence, strength and tenacity.

I admire your ability to set boundaries and boldly speak your truth.

I love how satisfied you are with your own company.

I am grateful that you feel safe asking for help and that you are so generous in giving help.

Your kindy teachers tell me that you'll be our Prime Minister one day, and sweetheart, you were born to lead.

So, Ellie, my prayer for you is to embody this wisdom and remain aligned to your true authentic self. Stay true to the you that's connected to everything and made in God's image—even if it means disappointment for others.

I pray that you approach all situations with compassion, understanding and peace in your heart.

I pray you have the strength and courage to overcome the inevitable hardships you will endure in your life, knowing that you are never alone.

Ashleigh Moreland

Finally, I pray that you know, feel and believe that you are loved, with every cell of your physical body and every part of your ethereal soul, for all of eternity.

There is nothing you can do, no mistake so big that would ever change your worthiness of this love.

You were born worthy.

Amen.

With all the love in the entire Universe and beyond,

Mummy.

Letters to my Daughter

Incredible Things

Jessica Russell

There are so many things I want to tell you about all the experiences life will bring.

But this is your life, and the lessons you face are yours, not mine. As much as I'd like to give you all the answers to life, I just don't have them all.

What I can do is tell you my story, and maybe you will find something that could help you on your own journey.

From a very young age, I could see things others couldn't, I understood things others didn't, and I sensed the energy of everything around me so powerfully it was scary.

Whenever I spoke about these things, it made people uncomfortable. So I learnt to keep it to myself.

For a long time, I didn't listen to my own inner voice, my intuition. I made so many mistakes, especially with relationships, because I just didn't know how to trust myself enough to know when something didn't feel right. Only time and experience can teach you that.

Mistakes are how we learn what we will and will not accept in our lives. They guide you to the life you were destined for.

Holding everything inside, the way I did for so long, caused me so much pain and anxiety. I was terrified of upsetting people, thinking
I'd lose them forever.

I didn't understand that by only doing what made others happy, I was losing myself. And the only way to find myself was to stand in my truth and just be me.

Jessica Russell

Those who see you and understand you will find you. And they will love you for who you are.

So my journey to find me, to remember who I was and why I was here, in this life, began.

I met your dad when I was eighteen, and he has been by my side through everything. He is my greatest love.

But I couldn't shake the feeling I was missing something, missing that connection, that bond that we share with other women, as soul sisters and as friends.

I began searching for other women like me to learn from, so I could finally begin to heal the wounds that time had left me with.

Finding my soul sisters was a huge part of my healing journey. Knowing who you can trust can be hard.

Having people in your life who you love and trust is what we, as humans, need most. We crave that connection. We need each other to love, support, and to guide one another through life.

I finally understood where I needed to heal. The majick and energy of creation are all held inside our bodies, within our sacred space, within our Wombs. It can offer deep healing for yourself, and for generations to come.

I studied Womb Massage and Reiki, and I began to remember what I came to this Earth to do.

Everything I needed was inside me, waiting for me, these gifts that I could share with the world, these gifts that I could share with you.

You'll grow, and you'll learn, and you'll find your truth. You'll make mistakes, and that's ok because that's how we learn what's right for us and what's not.

Some days you'll have all the answers, and some days you just won't know where to start. It's ok if you need space or just want to take your time.

It's ok to say YES, and it's ok to say NO. The choice is always yours.

Always listen and trust that you know, in your heart and deep within yourself. Try not to let that feeling pass without giving it your full attention. Your intuition is your guiding light.

When you feel it, and it's a full-bodied FUCK YES, go after it, grab it with both hands and give it everything you have! Once you know, you can't waste a single second on things not meant for you.

Letters to my Daughter

You'll know when it's not because you'll feel that full-bodied FUCK NO! You are meant for incredible things.

I have been so blessed to have a daughter as strong, as beautiful and as brave as you. You have shown me how to speak my truth and walk the path I was destined for.

I want you to know that no matter what demons I'm facing, I'll always be here to help you through whatever is going on in your life.

The last thing I want to tell you is this: only you know what's in your heart, what you truly want and need in this life. So stay true to yourself, always speak your truth with as much love and compassion as possible, and never try to be someone you're not. It just doesn't work.

Rebekah Rose

Daughters of Mother Gaia

Rebekah Rose

To my beautiful, powerful holders of love and light, my daughters. The daughters of the Great Mother Gaia,

Although you, my daughters, have not physically blessed this earth, I know you are here. Your souls and spirits live through me, within me, and around me as a constant guide and the most loving reminder. With every gentle gust of wind, every sunrise and sunset I experience, and every flower I witness bloom, I am reminded of what a sacred experience this life is. This world is a magical gift to welcome daughters.

The most divine feminine energy is rising quickly now, for she has been suppressed for too long. Her power, wisdom, guidance, and love are needed and welcomed into this world.

In ancient times, the wisdom of women, of the womb and the heart was so treasured. This embodied wisdom is the truest treasure. Although it seems many have disconnected, I believe now is the time to remember and embody this magic again. Know we can never lose it because it will always reside within us. Sometimes just know when to search a little deeper within, my love.

And in remembering this magic, a new way of living, a new earth and a new human experience shall be co-created by the world's women. A world that unifies the ancient ways with the current beauty in our modern world, allowing all that doesn't serve to fall away unattached. To make space to live from love, connected to our womanhood, our unique sacred healing power, as guardians of this beautiful place, The Great Mother, Mama Gaia, mother of all life.

Letters to my Daughter

When I think of what so many of our future generations of women will be able to experience and bring to this world, it truly excites me. It lights me up from the inside. It drives me to inspire and pave the way for an incredible group of souls to make their own unique way, their own mark, lessons and teachings on this place.

Oh, sweet daughters, when we bring awareness and heal generational trauma and limiting beliefs and connect to our inner truth, that's when I know you will live limitlessly. When we listen to our unique self-expression, not only listen but trust our intuition and woman's wisdom that's you will heal it, with it, through it and co-create a world of bliss, united in love with all other women.

You will effortlessly receive and trust the messages gifted to you from the divine. You will know that your worth and the worth of everything Mama Gaia created for this world is richer than gold. Although our physical world makes up a tiny fraction of who we are as beings of light, consciousness, and pure energy, the physical is still a sacred part of us. Enjoy every moment in this human experience.

So, stop and smell those roses. And I mean really smell them. Indulge the senses. Immerse yourself in the feeling of having your entire body gifted the scent of a flower. Feel the soft velvet petals touch your bare-beautiful skin. Stop and witness the beauty of the full bloom with complete presence. Sit in silence and listen often. Know that receiving is equally as important as giving. Stay grounded, rooted in your centre, yet always remain in flow with life.

Know that you are not only deeply and unconditionally loved, but that YOU ARE LOVE in its purest form. Living from and in the space of pure love is the most powerful thing a woman can do for herself, her daughters and everything around her.

If I can hope for just one thing for the daughters of our Great Mother to take away from my words, it's that you awaken to what an absolute gift it is to be a woman. So, activate your Kundalini and let it shine through your whole being with pure love.

You are perfect, whole and complete, always.

With all of my heart's love, always.

With so much Love

Melissa Lainer

You know, I always thought I'd have a daughter. It's just what I thought would happen, coming from a family of mainly girls. But instead, I was blessed with two gorgeous boys, and I wouldn't change them for the world. They are kind, gentle, strong and smart, and I love them more than anything.

Then why am I writing a letter to my daughter? You see, I discovered over the years that I am my daughter. I am the little girl that I was to love and raise. So this story is for her and for anyone who needs it.

When I was conceived, two souls released energy that sparked my life into being—pure energy, pure light, growing and developing. I was born into a world where I was lucky to be goo'd and gah'd over, loved and held. My light shone brightly. I lit up people's worlds. Free to be me, unconditionally. My radiant light was accepted in all its glory.

My light did not shine like this forever. Fractures created by experiences in life weakened my self-confidence, self-worth and self-love. Over time, I forgot how brightly I shone and my impact on people. I dimmed my light to fit in, be liked, accepted, loved and to be seen but not seen all at the same time.

Outwardly I portrayed a reasonably happy person. On the inside, it wasn't always the case. To the outside world, I was a planner, someone that was very organised, sometimes excessively so. What people didn't know was that this was a learned behaviour created through trauma. Without the forward planning, organisation, and awareness of where everything was and what was happening in the immediate and near future, I felt unsafe. I craved spontaneity, but for others to bring it to my life, it wasn't something I could indulge in myself. I longed for the freedom to just be in every moment. But I couldn't. If I did that, when I did that, something always happened where I was met with criticism, blame or disappointment. This was my interpretation of the situation, whether it was the intention of others or not. My whole being was triggered by these moments; they took me right back to the shattered, self-doubting little girl that was blamed for things that weren't her fault.

Thrust into the adult world far too young. Knowing things, a little girl shouldn't know. Seeing things one shouldn't see. Hearing things one shouldn't hear. Attempting to process things a little girl shouldn't have to process. Navigating a new world of her own, not knowing the lay of the land, attempting to hold everything together for everyone because she felt this was her job, confused about what was happening and what it meant, and why certain choices were made.

Powerless. Alone. Abandoned. Not chosen. Sad, angry and broken.

My light felt close to being extinguished. It was reduced to nothing more than a flicker until one day, I remembered. While there is much in life that we cannot control, our light, the one we are born with, is ours to shine and can never be extinguished. It is waiting for you to breathe into it, to set it ablaze by listening to yourself, backing yourself, trusting yourself and loving and accepting yourself. It is waiting for you to remember that you are powerful, magnificent, unique and perfect just the way you are. When you remember, your light will shine again, radiant in all its glory.

So, take a moment. Breathe into your heart space. Find your light that resides there. Sit with it and breathe. Sit, listen, feel, and breathe. Sit, listen, feel and breathe, and when you are ready, expand your light. Light up your life with all you desire. Find passion and purpose and all your unique gifts. One step at a time. Always knowing that this is your light, this is your power, and you can illuminate even the darkest of spaces just by being you.

Go forth and shine, beautiful soul. I'll be looking for your light.

My Beautiful Baby Girl

Cymon Cox

For my beautiful baby girl,

I am a far from perfect, Mumma.

I am a raise my voice, Mumma,
a lose my temper, Mumma
a say stupid things, Mumma
talk too much, Mumma
nag too much, Mumma
lecture too much, Mumma
get upset a lot, Mumma
doing the best I can, Mumma.
Sorry, there is no instruction book for this, Mumma.

But I am also your biggest and loudest supporter, Mumma,
your cherish every achievement, Mumma.
Your observe every milestone, Mumma
save every memory and memento, Mumma.
Setting you up for life, Mumma.
Always there for you, Mumma
no matter what, Mumma.
Protect you with my life, Mumma.
Love You Forever, Mumma.

Letters to my Daughter

I have been very blessed in my life to know what unconditional love and support feels like.

I have been lucky enough to know both my mother's love and her friendship, which is beyond precious to me.

You have heard me say many times, my joyful daughter, that my world would be complete if you loved me as much as I love my mum.

It is a love like no other.

But I fear I am not the mother I would like to be, and sometimes, I let us down.

Please know I am always trying, and some days, I am at my best.

But those other days, the days I'm not so proud of, I would ask for a little forgiveness as I try to make things right and learn a life lesson.

Please understand that you are on my journey as much as I am on yours.

We will live, laugh, love and learn amazing things together!

Hey, Baby Girl, have I told you today that I Love You? Xx

To my Darling Penelope

Kate Billen

To my darling Penelope,

I write this letter as a reminder that if you ever feel like you have lost yourself, you can always find your way back.

I first felt this strange familiar feeling, but I didn't know what it was all those years ago. It was a feeling I was unaccustomed to, yet at the same time, it felt like an old friend. You were only a baby of around five months. While I don't remember the exact moment it arrived, and perhaps it had tried to reveal itself previously, I had allowed myself to become so disconnected that I didn't recognise it. Or, maybe, it was because I had never been awakened to its existence. None of the women in my life shared the knowledge of its existence that I am aware. But I can promise you, my earth angel, I will not make this mistake with you.

As quickly as it came, I shoved it back. I didn't know what it was, but I did know that I was scared of it. So, I ignored it. I had absolutely no intention of acknowledging it, but the thing was, it kept showing up. It was persistent. Always creeping into my mind here and there over the years. Penny, I now know that it was my truth. It was my intuition, inner knowing, and the wild spirit in me, telling me, pleading with me, begging me to hear that this is not you. It kept saying to me, you are not this person, and you do not have to live this life that is not authentic to who you are and is not serving you.

When I began to acknowledge it, my perceptions shifted. Slowly at first, and it was scary, but then, quite abruptly, I saw my world differently. My perceptions completely shifted. This shook me to my very core. I viewed my relationships in an entirely different light than I had done previously. I could see that gradually, over time, my sense of self had eroded, and I had conformed to what others wanted and expected of me. It wasn't anyone else's fault because I allowed the silencing of my intuition. I held others' expectations and opinions of me higher and stronger than my own inner essence. I had listened to their criticisms and judgement and took them as being true for me.

And that intuition, that wild spirit that I now let thrive, had burnt down to nothing but cinders and ash. But you know the miraculous thing about awakening to your own truth and acknowledging that sacred intuition, that essence of self? It's that it never gives up on you. The fire that once burned within you, that wild spirit that was eroded into those cinders and ash, can be reignited, revived, and you can rise back up in its flames.

Cassey Crook

Dear Daughter

Cassey Crook

Dear Daughter,
   I want to pass on the wisdom I've acquired in my thirty-nine-year life journey.
   I hope to create new insights and seeds of remembrance within you.

You embody love. You are born pure. You are
loved more than you can ever imagine.
There is a spark that lives within you. It's powerful. A piece of the divine,
it shines as bright as all the stars. It's within each cell of your being.

It's the feeling of peace.
The longing for home.
It's your direct connection to all life.
It's found in presence, stillness and doing what you love.
It's within you always.
It carries your ancestors' wisdom.
It reminds you, you are the creator of your reality,
you are that powerful.
Every child is that important.

Not only are you connected to the source that lives within
you, but also to a life force that's all around you, Gaia.
She nurtures, nourishes, grounds, supports, heals and balances you.
Mother nature knows your name. She draws in the clouds and sends

Letters to my Daughter

butterflies to dance for you. She cleanses and purifies you in her oceans. She enlivens, inspires and motivates when the sun shines on you.

Gaia leaves you messages everywhere. She paints the rainbow to remind you of hope and to show you're a part of something beautiful. Birds dance and sing for you. Herbs, plants and flowers give you sustenance. Gaia gives you animals for connection, and angels drop their feathers to remind you of hope. If you look, Gaia's messages are everywhere.

Spirit and mythical creatures walk alongside you. Don't let your sight be limited by what you can see. There's magic all around you, hidden in unseen worlds. You are a part of this magic, and you are magical. The elves, unicorns, fairies, dragons and mermaids support you. Call upon them when you need protection. They are with your angels, walking beside you in your life. They are here to lift your spirits. They have magical powers.

Trust. Trust you and trust in the universe. Trust in Mother Earth. Respect her, and she will be one of your best friends. Love her as much as she loves you.

You are light in human form. You are a part of something ancient, alive and beautiful.

You are unique and have your own gifts and abilities.

Trust your instinct because it'll whisper the way.

Don't be afraid to face your deepest fears and feel all your emotions. When you allow yourself to feel your emotions, you'll find courage, bravery and growth.

Laughter is the best medicine. It will help you live longer.

Softness and gentleness are honourable qualities, and so are having solid boundaries. There are lessons in all your experiences. Finding these lessons will help with the pains of life you will experience. Forgive. Forgive yourself.

Dance, play and enjoy the ride called life.

Love is the most potent force in the universe. Love yourself first.

You are more powerful than you can ever imagine.

You are loved, adored, honoured and connected.

You are never alone.

A spark connected to a source lives within you, always.

You are a part of the magical force.

Your mum and dad cherish all you are.

We see you. We feel you. We hear you. We will always speak the truth and love you.

We believe in you.

You are deeply loved, by all.

Love your Mumma.

Letters to my Daughter

My Dear Maddy-Leigh

Rachael Bryden

To my dear Maddy-Leigh,

A gift is who you are to this world. You knew right from birth who you were, and I love that heartfelt truth you express daily. People that know you and any new souls that meet you say how you light up the world and bring an energy into the room that is infectious. In this human experience, I knew you were an old soul full of fire and zest from day one. It's like you had to do things yesterday, and you knew how to go about it before anyone showed you. Your determination has and is admired by me and others around you.

Little did I know the lessons and truths I'd be taught while raising you and your brother. I've always said children are a gift to the earth. We are here to guide them so they can spread their wings and leave their legacy.

I'm always so grateful the universe let our paths meet again, and you chose me to be your mum. To sign that soul contract is an honour. You are truly a gift. From the moment I first saw you to each day watching you grow into the young woman you are now.

You, Maddy-Leigh, were definitely a challenge with your independent personality. I've learned so much from being your mum and guiding you to harness your energy, and words and helping you learn to guide others. You're not just my daughter, you're a soul sister of the heart, too, and I believe in all you do.

Real beauty isn't only on the outside, it also radiates from the inside of those true to themselves. Keep speaking your truth and guiding others around you. As you have seen, you are a light in so many lives. The difference you make. The beautiful and different ways of being, and how you dressed since childhood did not go unnoticed. You can walk into a room and without speaking your presence is seen, and I love that!

There will be times in your life where you'll meet people, and they won't be your people, and that's ok. You'll still leave a mark on their lives, and they'll grow in some form for themselves, as you will, from meeting new souls who don't align. They'll be your teachers in ways you won't realise until you're older. You'll look back and see the path you took after meeting them and the lessons you learnt along the way.

We all learn from experiences with each other. Whether it's teaching us or teaching them, we can all achieve growth. Keep speaking your heart's truth in all you do and shining your light bright as we are all here to have this human experience. And what an experience it is! To learn, grow, and see the light and the dark in all aspects.

Be a part of a larger whole. Allow the integration of all we learn so we can pass on the knowledge, whether in words or vibration. To connect with others and our creative journey. To help each other along our paths and everything we undertake in this human experience. To be the master of Your own journey and raise Your vibration.

But most of all, follow your heart and what aligns for you, my beautiful daughter.

I will always be here holding your hand or watching you walk your path called life, and I'm always so very proud of you.

Love Your mum.

Letters to my Daughter

Dearest Kiah Sage

Shelley Brown

Dear Kiah Sage,

You are my delight. My teacher. My gorgeous girl. You are Sage in name and character. I knew you would grow and change our family. Unexpectedly, you grew and changed me.

I remember when you were born. 'It's a girl,' they said. 'Where did the red hair come from?' they asked.

'Did you take drugs when you were pregnant?'

'We need to do tests. She needs to be transferred to the children's hospital. It is only safe for her to feed through a tube. She may not even know you,' they said.

It was they who didn't know you. Your spirit and fiery determination hadn't shone through yet. I didn't really know you either, not then. I didn't fully embrace their medicalese, but I did worry and wonder. I doubted you, and for that, I am immensely sorry. I know better now. You taught me.

You shifted my idea of success and a 'good' life. Not by lowering expectations, quite the opposite. I realised boundaries and limitations set by higher education and a career in property investment had snuck into my psyche as measures of success. How did I not see contentment as the key aim of human existence? Connection, belonging and purpose. These create a beautiful and bountiful life—the kind of life you make for yourself. A unique path paved with heart and your innate ability to trust higher guidance. There is power in the pride you have in yourself.

Many may assume identifying you separately to your disability to be the kind, correct and comfortable course. You see it differently. Cerebral palsy and all of its gifts are a part of you. You identify as a disabled person, not to discomfort others, but rather with a deep understanding and acceptance of who you are. This is not to be overcome nor to draw pity. In your own words, my darling one, 'I proud my cerebral palsy. I think better because cerebral palsy.' Better because of, not in spite of.

As you pave your way into the adult world, I feel trepidation. As per usual, you don't. You may be anxious, but I see confidence too. As you plan, the world is readying itself. Extraordinary people travel before you, guiding the way. Your message, gifts, and spirit need to be seen and heard. Shout loudly, my sweet, for you show others possibilities. Other girls, other disabled people, other AAC communicators, other psychics, and other physicists will see you, and it will help them rise to their purpose. But don't do it for them or me, only do it for you. Follow your passions, and a fulfilled life is all yours.

Accepting help and support is not always my forte. So, watching you require support every day makes frustration bubble. It is mostly mine, though, not yours. You carry yourself through with grace. Know that your thoughts, actions, heart and body are yours. Give them freely when it feels right. Continue to ensure that those who support you understand and respect your autonomy. Consent is yours alone for the giving.

Of all the beautiful people you have guided to our lives, many have grown their angel wings too young. Such sadness stings our life. Time with you is a gift. In moments of fatigue or frustration, I think of friends who passed and tried not to wish our time away. Yet, there is also much joy. The richness of friendships and community you built holds us both through this change in life, not of life. Hot flushes are mine for quite a while yet, my young one!

The mindfulness you tiptoe on others' hearts is to be admired. But don't fear, you tell a gentle truth, and it needs to be heard. So have courage and speak. The ripple you make will be felt far and wide. Expectations will rise to meet you. Perceptions will change. So tell it, your truth.

For every accomplishment, you work harder and longer. Despite many gains, there is still a lack of understanding and access in our community. I don't assume to know what it's like to be you, my daughter. I walk alongside with pride and admiration. Stretch your living wings. And fly.

With all my love, Mum.

Letters to my Daughter

My Spirit Daughter

Gezzell Sabina

To my Spirit Daughter,

For such a long time, I thought I needed you to make me feel complete. I know, right! Giving that power to another being isn't always the best, hey? Had I not learnt anything? But still, I prayed and wished for somebody to take on my feminine legacy. Someone to be the emerging matriarch to guide and share the wisdom with the next generation of women in my lineage. Was I wrong in wanting that?

As much as I longed for you and would have welcomed you with open arms and an overflowing heart, Daughter, you didn't come through. Instead, it was I who stopped the lineage of trauma. I spoke the unspoken words, broke through the fears, and cried the tears to wash away the hurt of our ancestors. I was the one to heal the hurt while you held me in energetic connection, which allowed the pathway for your brothers to come through.

These two strong, beautiful and independent boys have the ability to be the balance. They embody both the masculine and feminine qualities this world needs now. Your brothers are here to bring their light to this world. I feel you help guide your brothers, who are here for me as much as for themselves. They are here for the women who are next in line. They support and hold them the next generation of women while they navigate their lineage pathways.

So beautiful, Daughter, I never saw you, and I never got to hold you. Yet, I wonder what you would have looked like? Would you have curious ocean-blue eyes like your daddy? The long-dark luscious hair like your mum?

Gezzell Sabina

Little freckles on your nose like your brothers and that beautiful smile that speaks of wisdom, strength and endurance that I dreamt of in a daughter. These visions of your earthly vessel still haunt me with the what if's.

I know there was a connection and a merging of us where I felt you come through. I'm sure I carried you in my womb for a brief moment. I hope you know how truly sorry I am for taking away your chance to cross over to this realm. That day weighs heavy in my heart and soul.

And if I can let you know one thing, that choice I made had everything to do with my position on that timeline and nothing to do with not wanting you. If you could see inside my heart, you would know that I was shit scared and a little (lot) weak. I'm sorry I didn't fight harder for you. I'm sorry I wasn't ready for you. You made me a soul carrier, and I wasn't strong enough to see it through.

It still saddens me that you couldn't stay, but I hope and feel that the encounter was enough of a lesson for us both. Enough to allow your soul to evolve and mine to heal.

I look forward to embracing you when I cross over, and I feel our connection again.

To my daughterless mother sisters: know that we are the warriors we have been waiting for to fix the fuck ups to raise our own vibration and if granted, the Warrior Men to support us amazing Warrior Women.

To the daughters who stay in the cosmic soup of life, I honour and respect you for allowing your fellow earth sisters to heal and grow and make way for such beautiful peace within their own hearts and souls.

With all my love,
Your Spirit Mum. xx

Letters to my Daughter

You are my Heart

Belle Verdiglione

Isabella, you are my heart.

I knew your soul before you were born. I had a vision of you with blonde-curly hair and deep-blue eyes. An image that didn't even seem real until you were born.

I know you are here to be my greatest teacher. You are a gift.

I love how you notice the smallest of creatures, like a teeny lizard sunbaking under a rock or a bee collecting its array of pollen, an insect wriggling on the ground.

You are one with nature, and I see you.

Isabella, you are made of stardust.

The starlight inside you is not of this earth. You are not of this earth, and with this comes knowledge from ancient times.

I want you to know that you are never too much, or too loud or too angry.

You are perfection.

Just as a sunflower doesn't compare itself to a rose, I want you to remember, always, that you bloom in your own way and never compare your light with anyone else's.

Embrace your wild and find what sets your soul on fire. If you do this, you will be your happiest.

Isabella, you are magic.

I know you are because I am too.

The whispers of your heart are calling to you, and you know a language not from this time. So trust yourself and nurture this gift.

With the help of your dreams, dragons and animal spirits, you can decipher what is said. These are your anchor points for this lifetime.

Even when you experience challenges in your life, I want you to know yourself inside and out.

Be your biggest fan, even if things feel hard.

When I am no longer in this physical world, I want you to remember that I am always in you.

I am energy, you are energy, and we are always one.

And so it is.

Letters to my Daughter

To My Loving Daughter

Raylene Joiner

A letter to my daughter,

The day you were born was the best day of my life. I named you Crystal because of the love I have for gems. I love the way they hold power, how they shine and how they make you feel. Before you were born, I knew I would name you Crystal because, my child, you were going to be something truly special and rare. You are like a gem, so beautiful and unique, and I know how lucky I am to have this chance to be your mother.

I am writing this letter to tell you just how much you have helped me change my life just by being born. You saved me from the destruction I once lived. See, for many years, I was homeless, living from couch to couch, place to place, not having any stability or responsibilities in my life. I constantly made bad decisions and had a poor me attitude and a victim mentality. I was abused and traumatised, and so in return, I abused others and hated who I was. There was no meaning in my life, and I didn't want to live anymore.

I didn't want to have any children for many years, as I thought how could I be a good mum to a child when I could not even look after myself. When I became pregnant with you, I wanted my life to be different. I was tired of the sadness and pain I suffered each day. I was tired of abusing alcohol and being addicted to substances, and I just wanted to feel my heart and feelings again. Since the age of twelve, I had numbed out my feelings.

When I was fifteen, I fled to the city and spent two decades just trying to survive, re-living my traumas every day. I had a story of sorrow and just wanted it to end.

Raylene Joiner

My loving and caring daughter, I did not understand what love was until the day I held you in my arms. I knew from that moment things in my life had to change for you to have a better life.

So from that moment on, I started breaking the chains of handed down generational patterns and family traumas. I have tried my best to give you the love none of my family was shown. All I ever wanted was to give you a better start to life than the rest of the family ever had.

I now take full responsibility for my life because I know who I truly am. I have seen my faults and worked on my shadow self. I have become a loving and compassionate person because of the love you have shown me. I have made up for my past mistakes, and I realise it is all because you saw my soul and loved me unconditionally.

You, my daughter, are so smart, funny, and caring and have the most beautiful-kindest soul. I want you to know that you can become and do anything you put your mind to. So, the best advice I can give you is what I wish I had been given as a teenager: your thoughts and intentions create your reality.

So, reach for the stars, my darling. Dream big beautiful one because you can do anything if you just put your mind to it. Seize every opportunity that comes your way, don't buy into the fear. It only makes you feel stuck. Give things a go anyway, even if it feels scary. Life is like a movie, and you are the main character.

So don't take life too seriously. Laugh out loud and remember what I taught you. Love everyone no matter what they look like or their religion or nationality. Be kind and generous and look after your family and friends. Be honest and trustworthy, use your common sense and trust your gut instincts.

One last thing I want to say is, thank you for choosing to come into my life and for loving me unconditionally. I love you with every part of my being and will be there for you no matter what.

Your Mumma.

Letters to my Daughter

My Baby Girl

Jenny Arnold

My mother was only sixteen when she had me. Teenage pregnancy was more unusual back then. I was bought up by my grandparents, mostly, who I adored. I don't remember my mother being around much until I was about four or five. I went from a safe environment in the English countryside to being in a terraced house with no home comforts or food and living with her boyfriend, who I now know as my abuser.

Over the years, I remember moving to different homes and being given food and safety by the neighbours. I played alone, and my only friends were tadpoles and frogs at the local pond. As a child, you float through life, and you don't understand what is going on. A child lives in a world of imagination. I know I did because it's all I had. Now I'm older, I assume he was abusing my mother too, but I never saw it. I only saw her cry with her friends. Maybe she wasn't strong enough to protect me. She never gave me answers, so I don't know.

I lived between 'home' and my grandparent's house on weekends and school holidays as I grew up. My mother liked her freedom and loved to party and spend time with whoever she was going out with at the time. I guess I realise now that's what a young adult is meant to do, and a child gets in the way. I always felt in the way. That life was normal to me. The feeling of loneliness and feeling left out was normal for me. I did not realise that disconnection and neglect from my parents as a young child affected me so deeply until later in life.

I've had counselling over the years. I tried to speak to my mother about our past and my abuse, which she brushed aside. She said she didn't know about it. I was told I was too sensitive and made to feel I'd made it up, so I bottled it up again, but my resentment grew against her. I withdrew from her. I built a brick wall. When I was sixteen, she had my sister. Their relationship was the way it was supposed to be, a mother-daughter bond so strong. But, of course, it was. She was present as a mother, and this baby was wanted.

I left and created my own life, living with different friends, and at nineteen, I became self-reliant and got my own place. I searched for the feeling of acceptance and love for years. I found it for a while in the rave scene. We were a crowd of broken people, all with common experiences and traumas. We lived as one family. We danced together, full of happiness, yes, it was drug-induced, but it felt amazingly complete at the time until everyone started to fall apart. Friends died, we grew distant from each other, and I was lost again.

At twenty-nine, I had your brother. I found the love I'd searched for. Becoming a mother was the best feeling I'd ever felt, and I knew I would protect it at all costs. However, my resentment deepened because how could a mother not want their baby? I felt so rejected by both my parents. This hurt was so deeply rooted in my heart. How could it ever be healed?

I eventually reconnected with your father. He was the greatest love of my life from my raving days. He was my soul mate. We made a home together. We were a real family, everything I dreamed of.

My girl, I dreamt about you. I knew I would have a daughter. Next, I knew your name and saw your blond hair. You came into our world and brought even more sunshine into our lives. You were both amazing kids, so funny and calm. I hope you feel you had a great childhood. I think I did my best. We've had our stressful times, and I may have been overprotective, but I had to be, you know that, right?

As young adults, you became individuals, as close as can be. That's all I could have asked for, and you're both so amazing. This is when I know I've done a great job as a Mother.

Deciding who you are has been hard for you. We embraced your decision. Of course, we did because we love you. You are finding your feet, becoming a beautiful woman, experiencing relationships, heartbreaks, and of course, my defences have been on high alert. I don't want anyone hurting you and making you feel how I have felt. But I've learnt to step back and guide you

Letters to my Daughter

to help you make your own decisions, which you are doing. I'm so very proud of you.

I've reached a stage in life where I've achieved a lot in self-reflection and healing. I've disconnected the cords of hurt I've carried. The heartache and challenges in my life have made me stronger, and I stand up more for what I believe because life is too short. No one will hurt me again. I know you've seen that change in me, and I've made you proud. I know my mother has to find her own healing. I cannot help her, I know it wasn't my fault, but I will not feel guilty for staying away. This is my self-preservation.

You and I have an amazing connection, I'm so thankful I have the mother-daughter bond I've always wanted, and it's truly unbreakable.

Thank you for coming into my life, my baby girl. I love you with all my heart to the moon and back. xxx

Conny Wladkowski

Spread your Wings & Fly

Conny Wladkowski

Dear future generation of amazing and powerful women,

I'm writing this letter to you about a topic very close to my heart, the fear of judgment and trying to fit in. This subject is close to my heart because I struggled all my teenage years, and I come across it with many teenage clients of mine.

Most teenagers feel like they don't fit in anywhere and worry a lot about being judged. They often don't like how they look and feel peer pressure to fit in.

So did I. However, no matter how hard I tried, I never fit in, and I was never part of the popular group of girls.

Working with teenagers, I hear about their struggles every day. Many don't like who they are. They worry about showing their true selves because they are scared of judgement. All they want is to fit in and be accepted. They are often so sad and angry. I just want to hug them and tell them they will be fine. I wish someone had told me that. I thought no one would ever like me for me.

As a teenager, I felt very shy and insecure. To the outside world, I was just 'uncool'. I had braces and hated the way I looked. I had no friends because they judged me for how I looked and for getting good grades. I was judged because I was shy. I felt so lonely and unliked.

My best piece of advice to you, the amazing future generation, my daughter, and my nieces is, don't worry about being judged and embrace who you are. When you are your true authentic self, you will feel happy, and you can thrive in life.

Letters to my Daughter

There are always people who will judge you. The mother who works full-time is judged for having her kids in childcare all day. The mother who doesn't work is judged that all she does is clean the house and cook. No matter what you do or who you are, people will always judge you. So you might as well be true to yourself and live your life the way you want to live it.

When you are your true self and come from your heart space, your tribe will find you. Those people who will matter in your life will unconditionally love you and be there for you through thick and thin. These are the quality people. Nothing is more freeing than just being who you are without any conditions on yourself.

Usually, judgement from other people reflects their insecurities and has nothing to do with you. So it's best not to let them get to you. I know it might be hard at first, but practise. The more you practise, the better you will get.

Also, accept other people for who they are with all their quirks and differences.

Lastly, don't put judgement on yourself. Love yourself unconditionally, which doesn't mean that you can't improve and grow. You can be a masterpiece and a work in progress at the same time.

Love yourself for where you are on your journey.

Dress the way you want to dress, listen to the music you want to listen to and speak from your heart. Once you live without the fear of judgement from others and yourself, you can shine your light, and the opportunities life gives you are endless.

Spread your wings and fly!

… Tracey Wilson

I Love You

Tracey Wilson

Dear daughters, children,

What a wonderful world we exist in here on earth. The beauty is profound. All people are rich with experiences, stories and tales, not just the interesting ones but also the quiet wallflowers. Their stories and emotions can run as deep as the deepest waters.

This world is full of polarities. Good, bad. Light, dark. Yin and yang. Look deep within yourself when times are tough and reflect. What is this teaching me? Why is this triggering me? Where does this trigger stem from? Find a new perception in the understanding of an experience. Find the positive and reframe the narrative you tell yourself. The stories you speak. This can be a challenge. But this is how we EVOLVE. You create new-positive healing pathways that restructure your DNA. If You EVOLVE, we as a collective, EVOLVE.

Healing must be sought in difficult times. If not to heal wounds, it manifests as stressors in your body and mind. These can stay with you your entire life. Sometimes dormant, waiting, and other times actively wreaking havoc.

You CAN heal yourself.

The human race craves more of us who live with integrity in all we do. People who live without projecting their wounds onto others. People who operate from a place of love and respect. Who trust their instincts and follow their truth.

With greater reflection, you will learn to trust your instincts. Your instincts, dear child, will always navigate you in the right direction. If you are willing

Letters to my Daughter

to listen, your body will tell you. Do you buzz with joy? Did you get a sharp ping in your chest? Did you find or recognise a red flag?

Let's speak of red flags. They are pointers, part of your internal road map for navigating this world, people, jobs, bosses, and relationships. Red flags at the start of a relationship of any sort DON'T go away. You can pretend like they're not there, but hear me right, they will ALWAYS come back to bite. However, you have a choice. You can find compromise in your red flag or recognise it for what it is and have the strength to take a different path. Sometimes the red flag is a limiting belief of our own.

It's ok not to get everything right. You're not meant to. No one is. Find perfection in the perfectly imperfect.

Be mindful of people-pleasing. Our society demands that we be good girls. Do as you're told. Don't like it, it doesn't matter because you need to do it. It is expected of you. You're obliged to do this. Let me tell you, dear child, you don't have to do ANYTHING you don't want to do. Be brave enough to say, 'No sorry, that's not for me,' and 'I don't feel comfortable with this,' and 'Thanks, but no thanks.' Or perhaps it needs a firmer 'NO!' It is harder to flow with your life's purpose when you are busy fulfilling everyone else's desires for you. Others have expectations of what they think YOU should be doing, in particular, to help them. But remember, people generally respect honesty and vulnerability when delivered respectfully.

You may wonder, what am I here for, why am I here? The answer to this will unfold with time. All you need to do is live your truth. Be unashamedly you, quirks and all, live from your heart. Follow your bliss. We don't have to be like everyone else. You are uniquely you, and you were born to be this way.

There is no need to have a desperate need for a partner. Divine timing IS a thing. Not everyone is to have the same relationship experiences and timings. Reframe the ending of relationships. An ending need not be hard when done from a place of truth and respect. Let go with ease.

When you live in your truth, you will attract divine humans into your life experience. Some are here for a reason. Some are here for a season. Some truly are meant to be around forever. No searching is required. Just acceptance for what is.

You will not get everything right. I certainly have not. However, these lessons I speak of I have learnt through experience. Through deep exploration of who I am and who we are as a species. These are things that I

Tracey Wilson

wished someone shared with me, so I could have been stronger, to stand in my power sooner.

    I have many more lessons to go, and these stories of guidance and wisdom, I'll embrace you with, my dear child, in my greying years.

    We will laugh, we will love, and we may cry, and it will be perfectly divine.

    I love you.

Letters to my Daughter

Charli Rose and Jade

Aimee Mitchell

I experienced an enormous contraction, closed my eyes, and witnessed the brightest-white light I have ever seen.

Time stood still, and I said out loud, 'She's an angel.'

My doula grabbed my hand and said, 'Yes, love, she is.'

To be honest, this response pissed me off!

Although it was apparent she was doing her job (agreeing to comfort), I felt the moment's magic was dismissed.

How the fuck was she to know I just experienced the essence of my baby girl's soul, her pure-angelic energy surrounded me in a split second.

I will always remember that heavenly moment.

Before falling pregnant, I spent years battling crippling depression, anxiety, and suicidal tendencies. I was addicted to finding ways of escaping my painful reality through partying and heavy drug use. The minute I knew you were growing in me was the second the universe decided to guide me away from destruction.

Charli Rose Faulkner
Born on the 26 January 2015 at 8:13 pm.

Not only did you bless me with the gift of becoming a mother, but you also showed me how to love unconditionally and inspired your dad and me to choose a better path for ourselves.

The instant you were Earth-side, you brought light and joy to the entire family. Your gentle-caring nature, loving heart and true wisdom have been evident from the start.

You are exactly what the world needs more of, and as you grow, your natural ability to lead by example shines.

And then there were 2…

Jade Moizelle Faulkner

Born on the 3 June 2019 at 10:44 pm.

Throughout my pregnancy with you, Jade, I was shown a new way forward regarding healing. Past life regressions, ancestral DNA clearings and learning about cellular memory became profoundly intriguing, and I found myself attending several Merkaba activations. I specifically remember the activation I participated in on New Year's Day 2019. The facilitator was doing a headcount of attendees before we commenced the meditation and was becoming confused as she kept counting one more person. She soon realised it was your presence. You were in utero and had guided me there.

The message you were transmitting was impossible to ignore. It was time for me to step up! Time to take myself seriously and truly begin my journey of self-discovery to take charge and honour our ancestors while initiating a brighter future for us and all the generations to follow.

As you grew in my womb, the energy I felt was strong and direct, a true reflection of your personality today. You are fearless, deeply compassionate, loyal and confident. You know what you want and how to get it.

It is obvious you are in this world to make an impact! You have a strong sense of who you are!

Charli and Jade, as parents, we never expected to bring the world such a powerful duo. We are so grateful to be the ones that help guide you through this crazy world and are deeply humbled and honoured to learn the lessons each of you teaches us along the way.

Charli Rose

Smart, creative, beautifully sensitive with a heart of gold, the world can be a harsh place, so please do not let this harm your kind and genuine spirit.

Letters to my Daughter

Stand in your power, and do not be afraid to speak your truth. Your words matter and can help others create positive change in a world in need. Never lose your sense of humour and passion to create.

Jade Moiselle

To our brave, self-assured little in-house comedian, Jade, never let the fire in your belly reside. As you continue to learn the world's ways, your clever wit and ability to make light of any tough situation will continue to teach you patience through times of frustration. It is clear you have a mission in this lifetime, and we are so excited to watch this unfold.

Our promise to you both is to continue becoming the best versions of ourselves, to consciously nurture all the amazing traits you each hold in order to allow you guys to follow your dreams. Always know Dad, and I will never stop being your biggest supporters. It is a true honour to hold your hands through all the ups and downs life will throw our way. Words will never describe the love we have for you two. We got you!!!

Love forever, Mum.

My Darling Heart

Emma Fedigan

Darling heart,

You were brought into this world not by chance but by breath, soft kisses, heaving-bare chests, stardust, magic, moonbeams, planets and chaos.

I wish when I started my journey of understanding the infinite universe that is me, someone gently pulled me aside and said, 'Em, let's have a cuddle'.

I am cosmic dust growing into the incredible universe.

As I sit with what feels like a suitcase's contents spread before me, I can't help but feel robbed of some important things I should have been told. Today, I vow to share what I have learned so my struggles, bleeding heart and crucifixions will not be in vain. I promise you that yours won't be either, but I hope I make them lighter for you to carry. I hope to free you of the excess luggage you carry that isn't even yours.

I'm sending you a crone with long-dark hair, leaves, earth and twisted branches weaved throughout, and in her soulful eyes, a sparkling galaxy. Her skin is soft, mapped by travelled journeys she has walked. Lumps and bumps on her face have seen eons of change, with high cheekbones and plump cheeks that have held tears. Her arms seem frail but are strong and encompassing. Her bosom is round and soft, filling the space to rest your head on—a lap that is safe, warm, open and inviting.

She pulled me into her great-big, nurturing arms, and the discussion went kind of like this…

To do the work, you need to find yourself.

This means stripping bare of so many layers—not one of the expectations given to you is yours.

Letters to my *Daughter*

It's honestly the toughest fucking walk you will ever do, my darling. It's not fun, not fluff. It's not spiritual. It's mountains of grief that can come out as anger, hurt, fear, anxiety, chaos, hellfire and torrential rain. It's mountains to climb and sharp fucking jagged rocks you will slip down and re-open wounds. Everything will seem like it's fallen away, and it does and needs to for the most part.

Expectations and realities ebb and flow, and sometimes your world tips upside down and your entire existence lies before you.

But then the Crone cups your round face and says, 'Darling woman'.

It's in this moment where you have a choice to pick yourself up and carry on or not. If you carry on, you choose which bits to take with you.

There will be learning, and there will be how and why and tears, tears, my beauty, that will seem never to end. Hearts will break shatter, but these will be yours, and they will rebuild but will forever be changed. It is one of the loneliest isolating walks you will ever take. It will be a weight with generations of thick mud to wade through. Sometimes you might drown in it.

You will walk through eons of darkness with brief fragments of light. GRAB them, hold them, place them in your jar and keep walking through the dark. Those little lights will guide your way. I promise she, they, I will be here even though you won't be able sometimes to feel me or hear me. Keep going. Keep going.

You are stronger than you know.

As you grow, evolve and shift, you, and those around you will realise you are changing, and you may not be the same person.

The things you used to tolerate will become intolerable. Where you once remained quiet, you are now speaking your truth. Where you once battled and argued, you now remain calm and composed.

You now know your voice. Some situations no longer deserve your time, energy, or focus. So let them go, darling. We want you to strive for the inexpensive matter.

Anytime you choose yourself, you choose to grow, you're going to lose something, a part of you that you no longer need, and possibly people who no longer understand you or your needs. Those who may have had their own expectations about what you were to be or give them. You're losing habits and behaviours that you're no longer comfortable with.

Emma Fedigan

Growth is when we experience our feelings and emotions, but we don't let them control us. Stepping back and looking objectively, we can let go and accept things we cannot change. We detach from situations, people, behaviours and choices. We cannot be responsible for others' emotional work.

Be mindful and hold your boundaries. Listen to your body and your emotional wellbeing. You have a responsibility to choose how you act as well as react. Step away from harmful cravings.

The detachment is a deep breath of understanding and acceptance in response to that which is being expressed.

You're going to ruffle feathers, and you're going to lose those who feel they can't keep up. It is NOT your responsibility to solve others. You are responsible for yourself.

Love yourself and only you, first and foremost, always.

Letters to my Daughter

You Belong Always

Amanda Scott

As I feel the disconnect, myself included
the busy hum of what's left to do, the upcoming important bullshit
addicted to the numbness the checking out
fight and flight fluctuating with complete exhaustion
longing for something that can't be bought
Being afraid of messing it all up just messes it up
I am sorry, my love, so much wasted time
I am here now
Grounded
I see the love in your eyes
I see your beauty
Nothing is more important than you
So loved
You belong always
Always enough
Always worthy
ground and rise.
Present

My Beautiful Daughters

Jenny Stanley-Matthews

Dear Petrice and Giselle,

I was a tomboy who believed boys had all the good stuff.

I watched my brother receive remote control toys, things that lit up and made noise and most of all, a skateboard.

My parents refused to buy me a skateboard, but I was determined to have one. I started off wearing one rollerskate and pushed along the gutter to get the same effect until I saved up enough pocket money to buy a cheap fibreglass skateboard.

My sister and I received Barbie dolls which my sister loved, but I thought they were a waste of time because they did nothing. I sent a subtle message one day by hanging my Ballerina Barbie from a noose above my bed. Not very grateful, I know, but I don't think anyone gave me more dolls after that!

I wouldn't classify myself as a women's libber; however, I recognised injustices between the sexes from a very young age. When I found out what 'periods' were and how long they were going to be a part of my life, I was livid, and don't even talk to me about the shock of seeing a video of childbirth in year seven.

I felt so ripped off to be born female!

Trying to navigate my growth with a chauvinistic father and sexual discrimination within the workplace during the 80s and 90s was challenging in itself. However, my attempts to be recognised for my intelligence, talents, and skill was like being in a pinball machine bouncing from one experience to another. My determination to stay in the game and be taken seriously inevitably left me white-knuckled, holding on to the flippers. I felt like

Letters to my Daughter

I always needed to prove myself so I didn't fall into the pigeonhole that pretty-blonde females apparently belonged in.

I have to admit, though, I played a good game. I even got bonus points for each lesson I found within my challenges. I learned to recognise and embrace the power of my feminine energy and womanhood. Just when I was starting to feel confident within my pinball game and saw my name in lights as a *'high scorer'* I had you, and the game went to the next level, got faster and different rules now applied.

It was one thing for me to learn through my experiences and become an avid player of the game, but I wanted you to have a gentler experience and be cushioned by some of the wisdom I could give you. I encourage you to embrace your feminine energy in all of its magnificence and, unlike me at your age, recognise the power you have within you.

Wisdom has taught me MY responses, biases and limiting beliefs helped fuel the outcomes I received in life. I want the best for you girls and your brother, and I want all your dreams to be within reach regardless of your sex. I guess that I have always wanted, even as a child, to be seen as human and not a stereotype.

Being your mum is the most important role I will ever have in life. The responsibility that I have felt in protecting, nurturing, and helping you develop into the beautiful, strong, compassionate, and intelligent adults that you are, has been the scariest and most rewarding experience. Sometimes, I have been too much, sometimes I have probably not been enough, and every now and again, I got it just right because when I knew better, I did better.

If I were to hand over some wisdom, it would be not to give your power away. It took me a long time to realise how many ways I donated mine to gain acceptance and approval. I gave my power away to friends, family, my body image, my relationships, my job, and the list goes on. You are powerful, and when you value and nurture that power, you will attract people, relationships and an environment that is your vibrational match and all the goodness and love you deserve.

I'm scanning the world to find fragments of me
That I gave away so they'd like what they see
I know that I now have to love myself first

Jenny Stanley-Mathews

To embrace my power to find my self-worth
I now recognise all the great things I do
I've regained my passion
I'm no longer blue
I'm happy and content within my own skin
I'm excited. I'm radiant
Let my new life begin!
I inhale a breath and make life start
It fills up my lungs and reaches my heart
I accept life with grace, joy, and ease
And release all no longer needed to the caressing breeze
I am a daughter, a sister, a mother, a wife
I am grateful for all my roles in this life
And I'm mindful to always appreciate me
As I look in the mirror, I love what I see

To my beautiful daughters, my wish for you is to look in the mirror and always love what you see. Mum xxx

Letters to my Daughter

You are Always Loved

Kristie Inker

The breeze picks up, and the cooler air circles our warm bodies. The sun sinks lower in the sky, beginning its descent behind the horizon. It's no longer day but not quite night. It's that magical time where a strange calm washes over you and the day's worries disappear.

Even if a single soul didn't witness its beauty and admire its resilience for rising time and again to see a new day, the sun would still rise tomorrow. If this was the last sunset we celebrate together, I hope you continue to shine like the sun and have the resilience to rise every day despite the worries you carry from the day before.

Between sunrise and sunset, there will be laughter and tears. There will be unwashed hair days and cereal for dinner nights. There will be celebrations of academic achievement and the wonderful, gooey, heartwarming delight of new-found friendships. There will be broken hearts and promises that will feel like the world's end, but tomorrow, the sun will rise again.

The tides turn, the winds change, and darkness replaces the light in the sky. Creatures stir from their spaces and begin the next part of their journey, scurrying along the sand and playing in the shallow-calm waters. So many beautiful and magical moments are missed if you focus on the darkness around you and don't pause to admire the tiny things that make up life's larger picture.

The gulls leave the beach and soar along the coast to settle for the night. You dig your toes deeper into the soft-clean sand and take a deep breath of fresh air. A small crab cautiously scuttles between rocks and makes its way to the shore, where it busily works burying itself. Finally, the crab emerges from its sand shelter, sensing danger has passed, and continues towards the water. No one told the crab to hide. Instead, it learnt through life that trusting its instincts will keep it safe from harm. In the same way, it knows you can't truly live life if you stay in a sheltered space all the time.

The tides ease into their positions, and the soft breeze mingles with the sound of gently breaking waves, no more than a faint drumbeat. No more creatures frolic at the water's edge, but the stars begin to pepper the dreamy hues of the night sky. You can feel a sense of calm. The day's busyness has washed away. Even though it's dark, your senses tell you nothing exists now that didn't live in the light. Nothing here will harm you, and you can sit safely knowing that it's ok to be still.

There is no need to be doing and going all the time. There is a time for rest and reflection in every day. Look to the moon for inspiration. It illuminates a fraction of the darkness but reflects so peacefully on the water. It lights the way for others who need guidance while seemingly doing very little.

My beautiful Earth Angel, there is no worldly advice I can give you, even after my many years of experience on this Earth. Life lessons are not something I can teach you. Your life lessons will be different because they will come from living your own life. Your choices will always lead you to where you are right now. This moment will exist because you followed this path, and that's ok because you're far from the end of your journey. Make choices today. If they are good, then celebrate them. If they are bad, make new choices. The sun will rise again tomorrow.

Sleep well, precious one, knowing you are always loved.

Letters to my Daughter

Feel the Joy of Life

Marie Czatyrko

In her later years, I spent time with my mother, Albina, and realised we had an unbreakable bond. How much heartache did I cause her? I'm an identical twin, so Albina laboured twice at my birth. She was forty and an educated woman for her time after surviving the Second World War. Anthony, the man she was to marry, was killed.

When my mother told me their story, I felt she still loved him. I believe he was waiting for her at the end of her bed when she passed. Around the time Anthony died, my mother also lost her brother when he volunteered and fought in Franco's war in Spain. A battle she described as the *'unnecessary war'*. Perhaps to survive, Albina agreed to a marriage of convenience.

Trauma after trauma.

She spoke about her mother's love, something I only understood after having my first daughter, Bianca. Due to congenital glaucoma, Bianca was born blind. However, against all odds, nine years later, I gave birth to my second daughter, Eva. Bianca was present at Eva's birth. This gave them an unbreakable bond. Siblings. Sisterly love.

Both my daughters have had a life of learning. Eva was only nine when she was diagnosed with type 1 diabetes. A lifetime sentence to inject insulin daily, measure blood sugar levels and decide which food to manage. Each has experienced their share of heartache. I have nurtured, loved, and doted on them. As with my mother and I, the bond with daughters is also unbreakable.

I have been active and present in understanding the traumas passed down from generation to generation. However, the cycle stops here because

Marie Czatyrko

Bianca and Eva have decided not to have children. However, they do have animals they have bonded with, babies who are feathered, fluffy and cuddly. Three cats, one dog and two birds are our family members. I can feel their motherly love for each of their babies. I also have nieces and nephews who have children but have had the trauma of their great-grandparents passed down to them.

To describe love, one can only measure the ways in different forms.

When eight and a half months pregnant with Bianca, I was left by her father. This abandonment and then giving birth to my blind child, who I love dearly, was a challenging stage in my life and created much trauma. It meant challenges were met and dealt with alone. It meant medical decisions about Bianca were made alone and without anyone's permission or support. I learnt to forgive myself for feeling hurt, betrayed, and angry. I stopped blaming Bianca's father for my troubles because I realised he had his own trauma. We remained friends.

Then, just when I thought I'd mapped my life path decisions, I met Christopher, Eva's father, a man who fell in love with me and proposed on our third day. We married six months later.

Along with Bianca, Christopher's parents, Halina and Kostek, were also present at Eva's birth. Like my parent's they too survived the Second World War. Their love was unconditional, sharing both time, stories, and skills, teaching the piano, how to cook and how to knit.

Eva's grandfather was in the Polish resistance. He reminded me of Ian Flemming's James Bond. He was reserved and quiet, traits which his granddaughter also has. Family is magical and means evolving with each new member.

As a child, I wish my parents had advised me to be myself, be happy and follow my heart. But how could they? They weren't given this advice because survival was their priority.

My biggest life lessons are forgiving and letting go of hurt, accepting that challenges can build character, and learning to adapt because change is good.

In the quiet mornings, I think of the message of love I will leave both you and my family. I listen to the birds sing and ponder and include distant relatives and those who are not blood relatives but are family, nevertheless. They are in my thoughts and my love.

Letters to my Daughter

Strength, courage, bravery, togetherness.
Feel the joy of life.
Breathe the air of motivation.

I look up at the sky, up at the stars and imagine the many heartbeats a mother's love has for her children if the measurement of her love was distance. Going to the moon and back is but a moment in a mother's time loving her children.

Always remember the laughter, hugs, peace and happiness.

Love,
Ma xxx

A Loving Mum

A Letter to Your Daughter

A Loving Mum

Letters to my Daughter

A Loving Mum

www.ingramcontent.com/pod-product-compliance
Lightning Source LLC
Chambersburg PA
CBHW020326010526
44107CB00054B/2003